THE ART & EMBROIDERY OF JAN MESSENT

CELTIC, VIKING & ANGLO-SAXON EMBROIDERY

Acknowledgements

I am deeply grateful for the enduring belief of the Editorial Director, Roz Dace, and my editor, Katie Sparkes, at Search Press, that I could still produce a book of this sort after a lapse of many years. Their faith in me, their assurances and help, enthusiasm and interest in the project have made my efforts so pleasurable and worthwhile. More than that, however, has been their expertise in presenting my material to advantage while being sympathetic to my personal views; the kind of collaboration of which an embroiderer usually only dreams. Thank you also to the rest of the Search Press team, whose skills went into making this book so special for me: to the visionary designer, Juan Hayward, and to the superb photographer, Gavin Sawyer.

Jan Messent. Hampshire, England. 2009.

THE ART & EMBROIDERY OF JAN MESSENT

CELTIC, VIKING & ANGLO-SAXON EMBROIDERY

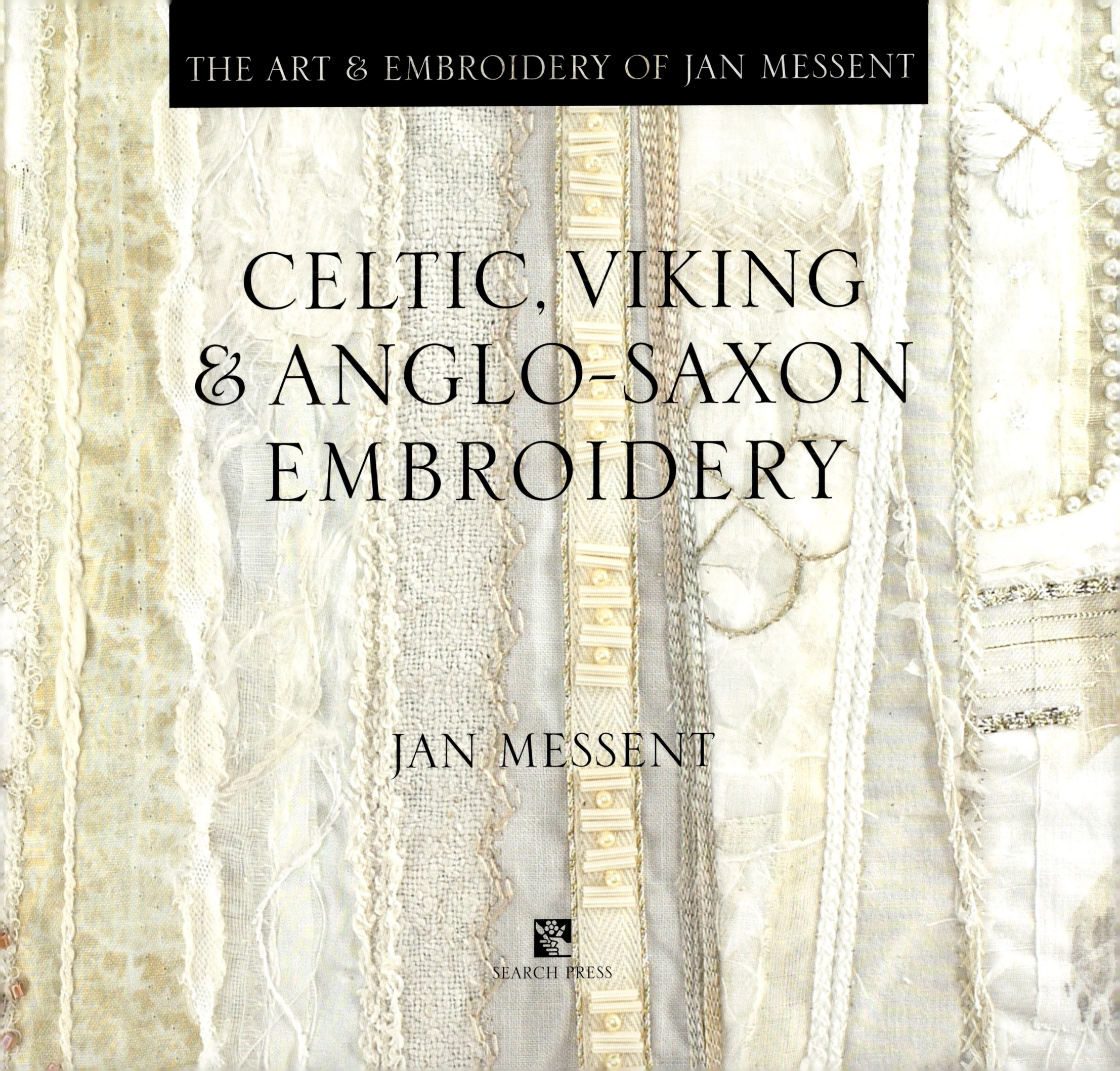

Jan Messent

Search Press

First published in Great Britain 2010

Search Press Limited
Wellwood, North Farm Road,
Tunbridge Wells, Kent TN2 3DR

Reprinted 2010, 2011

Text copyright © Jan Messent 2010

Photographs by Roddy Paine Photographic Studio

Photographs and design
copyright © Search Press Ltd. 2010

All rights reserved. No part of this book, text, photographs or illustrations may be reproduced or transmitted in any form or by any means by print, photoprint, microfilm, microfiche, photocopier, internet or in any way known or as yet unknown, or stored in a retrieval system, without written permission obtained beforehand from Search Press.

ISBN: 978-1-84448-409-6

The Publishers and author can accept no responsibility for any consequences arising from the information, advice or instructions given in this publication.

Printed in China

The image on the right is a detail from 'King Eadward's tunic', seen on page 92. Far right is a detail from 'The Book of Ancient Accessories' (see page 98).

BEOWULF English poem, written between 680 and 800, describes Tapestries, worked in gold, glittering on the walls, many a fine sight for those who have eyes to see such things.'

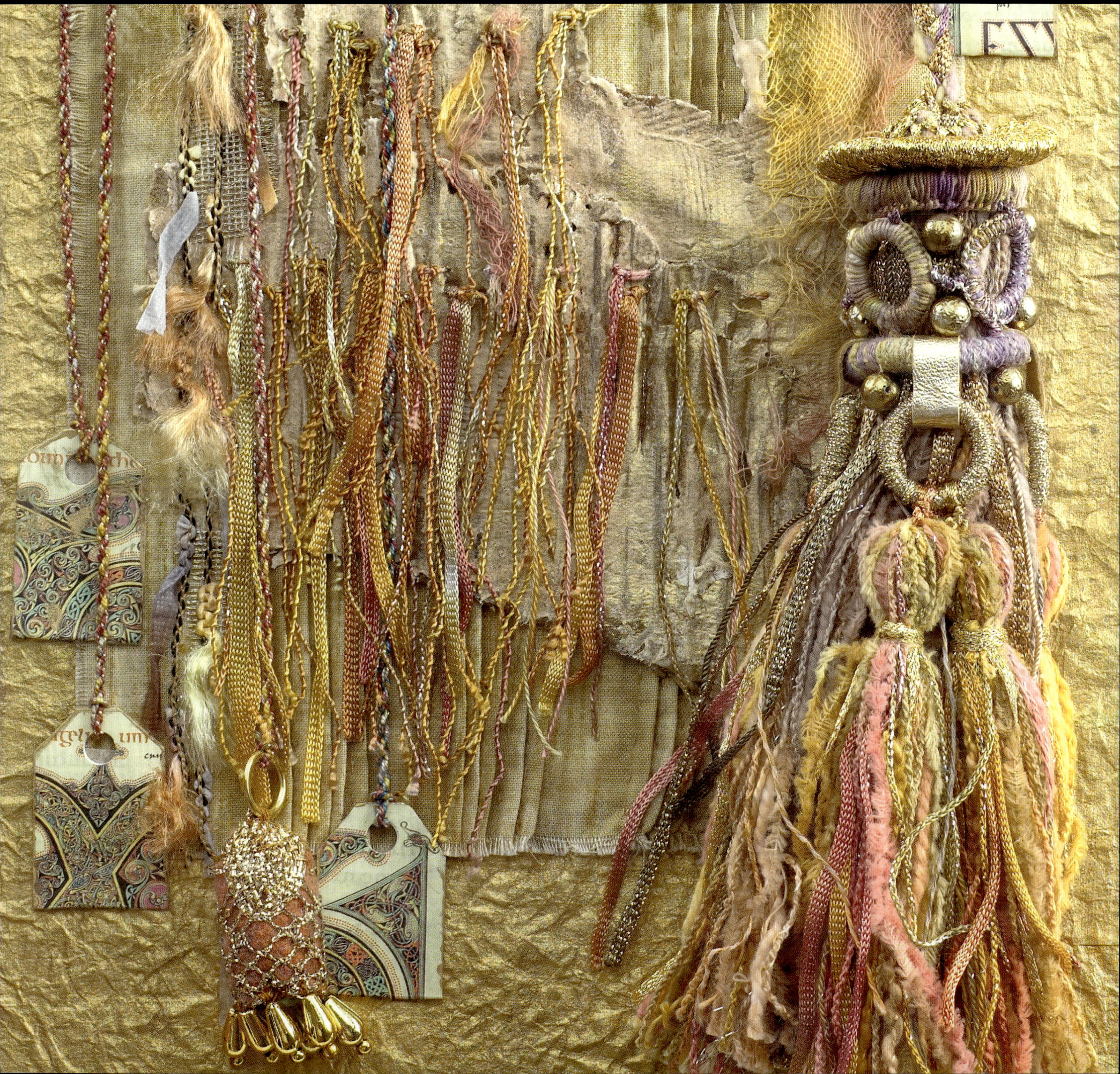

CONTENTS

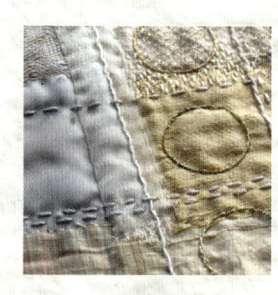

INTRODUCTION 8
A brief historic survey 12

CELTIC INFLUENCES 16
The needlecase 28
St Dunstan 32
Wulfwynn, Abbess of Romsey 33
Leofgyth of Knook 33

THE BOOK OF STITCHES 34

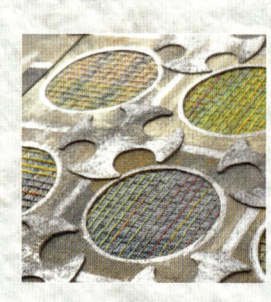

THE BAYEUX STITCH BOOK 52
The Bayeux Tapestry box 70

THE DRESSING-UP BOOK 74
King Eadward's tunic 92
Green sleeve fragment 93
Aelfreda's Gown for Feast Days 94
Aethelstan's Sunday-Best 95

THE BOOK OF ANCIENT ACCESSORIES 96
Ancient beads 100
Anglo-Saxon fragments box 102
Purses and pouches 104
The lucet 105
Four Anglo-Saxon purses 106
The workbox book 110
The woven notebook 111
Scissors case and needlecase 112
Shoes and two figures 116
King Harold's cloak for Hastings 117

THE BOOK OF MOTIFS 118
St Cuthbert project 132

THE DOMESDAY BOOK 138

INDEX 142

INTRODUCTION

I was never a large-scale artist. Fascinated by detail since I put on my first pair of spectacles at the age of eight, I have always felt more comfortable working smallish. Not miniature, but cosy. There have been a few exceptions like the Bayeux Tapestry Finale and the quilted St Cuthbert hanging (see pages 134–135 and 82–83 respectively), but the former was dictated by history and the latter was embroidered in small pieces, assembled afterwards. For a variety of reasons, physical, psychological, domestic and practical, I now prefer to make not only small pieces but unfinished ones too, experimental samples and easily handled bite-sized things that satisfy my curiosity and my senses without the accompanying performance of finishing, fixing or framing. Time is not the issue. Small things can take as long to make as large ones, depending on the technique, which, in my case, is hand-stitchery.

My enjoyment of hand-stitched techniques harks back, I think, to those very early contented days when, as a small child in the war years, I was taken regularly to a haberdashery shop that was closing down and where, up some dark stairs to a storeroom, my mother and I would drool over cards of ribbons and tapes, buttons and threads. There were mountainous stacks of cloth, yards of elastic, boxes of artificial flowers and feathers for hats, knitting needles and crochet hooks, black packets of sewing needles, wooden bobbins of silk, cotton and linen, shelves of old patterns and the warm aroma of fibres. Sadly, my mother's needs were for the functional

King Eadward's Pall

Measuring about 12in (30.5cm) square, this embroidery is derived from the funeral scene from the Bayeux Tapestry shown on page 124. Appliqué in natural fibres, satin stitch, whipped running, stem and Bayeux stitch.

rather than the ornamental, and embroidery lay undiscovered for me until much later. She did, however, bring home piles of old fashion magazines, already decades out of date, and I would puzzle at the contorted corsetted bodies and patent-leather hair which were, at four years old, outside my experience.

Nevertheless, I was taught early on how to sew by hand and machine, a Singer treadle, and those flowing swathes of fabric, the floating paper patterns and the crunch of scissors, the neat hems and buttonholes, the quiet clock-ticking hours of being alone with my imagination (while giving the appearance of industry, you understand), and having my mother's undivided attention (I had two older brothers) were a joy to me rather than a drudge. It was the first stirring of creativity I can actually remember, drawing and writing hardly qualifying, for I cannot remember not doing them.

Even so, few people regarded household needlework as being particularly creative. We all did it. If you wanted clothes, you made them. My father learned how to cobble, everyone made rugs, knitted and crocheted, quilted and patchworked, dolls were made from scraps, swimwear was made with the new shirring-elastic from surplus parachute nylon. Spare my blushes and don't ask what happened when said costume filled with North Sea water. Hand-sewing held no fears for me, but embroidery stitches in uniform rows never fired my enthusiasm, and it was not until I had children of my own that I discovered what else could be done with lazy-daisy and whipped running stitch other than to decorate my school cookery apron.

In retrospect, it becomes clear that those practical and resourceful times in which I grew up must have influenced the way I am working now. After a professional lifetime of producing embroideries-for-a-purpose, for exhibitions, commissions, for books, teaching and lecturing, I now have the time and a little more skill to follow my own personal inclinations. Now I can revert to those less hectic days of contemplative sewing, drawing, painting, researching history and embroidery, combining the results in a collection of handmade books instead of storing them away in boxes.

This latest phase in my development seems to have coincided with the recent renaissance of sketchbooking, journal-keeping, scrapbooking and personal book-making. I learnt basic book-making at college, but never like this. 'Altered books' would, I think, have been condemned by my tutors, since all books were precious even if you didn't like them. Needless to say, I have embraced this recent trend with enthusiasm, seeing it as a way of collating and presenting what I have learned and loved in a form that is both attractive and accessible. There are now some excellent books on the market dealing with all aspects of personal mixed-media book-making which are perfect for textile artists.

My first attempt at an 'altered book' was made to accompany a Regency novel I was writing whose heroine was a York milliner and mantua-maker. I knew she would have kept a book of samples like those kept by weavers, wall-paper makers and tailors, like those that had fascinated me in that musty upper storeroom. So I created one for her, sticking, pinning, matching samples of lace and velvet, silks, printed muslin and calico. I cut pages out (horror!) and replaced them with prettier ones, I painted over text and dismal photographs, slashing and burning edges and decking them with ribbons and labels. Then I re-covered it with bright embossed papers and tied it with buckles and cords. I was hooked!

I followed that with a subject close to my heart, the Anglo-Saxon period of English history, particularly its embroidery, combining all my favourite things: embroidery, writing, artwork, history and books. Naturally, one book could not hold all that. Besides, embroidery takes up more space than text and diagrams. So it would have to be several, one for each topic, including the history of embroidery, stitches and techniques, fabrics and threads, dyes, function, fashion and designs. And why stop at Anglo-Saxon when this period was influenced by Celtic design and, in its turn, by the Vikings of Scandinavia?

Detail from King Eadward's Pall, shown on page 8.

My old friends from Search Press came over for lunch: they're much closer to where I live now than they used to be. 'What are you doing these days?' they said. So I showed them, having just finished project number two. 'Ah,' they said, eagle-eyed, 'there's a book here, isn't there?'

'Yes,' I said. 'Probably.'

So my Search Press project developed into a work of sheer self-indulgence reflecting my interests more closely than a mere teaching manual would do, which has been the way of things in previous books. I make no apologies for hopping blithely through several hundred years without due regard for the many national and regional changes. This is not that kind of book. Nor is there much in the way of diagrams, instructions or lists of requirements. But because teaching skills are hard to shake off, it is inevitable that some explanations have crept in, here and there, about how a particular effect was achieved, usually much simpler than it looks and particularly aimed at those of us who enjoy hand-sewing.

Each of the small Books within this single volume represents a chapter that follows on, with overlaps, from the last. At the same time, I have aimed to illustrate various methods of making a sketch-/workbook as a way of keeping theme-based material together and to present working methods and designs to an examiner. Inevitably, each Book offers only a brief glimpse of a topic, because several volumes would have been needed to say it all. There is so much material; I had to be selective.

I have also aimed to draw attention to the centuries-old tradition of embroidery in England which has served as a foundation for present-day excellence. Early embroidery is still marginalised in books on Anglo-Saxon arts and crafts despite its exceptional high standard, so this attempt to redress the balance is my way of paying tribute to those Celtic, Anglo-Saxon and Viking women whose skills have seldom been recognised. Even so, I have been selective rather than comprehensive.

My system of measurements reflects the early one of inches that preceded the Continental metric system. So, since we are dealing with the past, I have chosen to place the inches before the centimetres, contrary to the usual practice. Originally, an inch was the length of the first (top) joint of the thumb, hence 'rule of thumb' meaning a quick estimate. A foot (twelve inches) was the average length of a man's foot, presumably wearing boots. So much for our smaller ancestors. A yard (thirty-six inches) was the length of a man's stride. Fabrics and threads were measured in ells, but this varied according to the material and its place of origin. Originally though, an ell was the length of a man's outstretched arm from shoulder to fingertip, hence our word 'elbow'. No wonder the measurement varied so much.

A selection of the Books I have created for inclusion in this volume. They are, from bottom to top, The Bayeux Stitch Book (page 52), Celtic Influences (page 16), The Dressing-up Book (page 74) and The Book of Stitches (page 34).

The Isle of Lewis Queen
10 x 7in (25.5 x 18cm)

On a cotton background, the chequered pattern is worked in Bayeux stitch outlined with couched gold thread. Stranded cottons and linen threads predominate. The figure is couched, including the face and hands, except for the central panel of long and short stitch and the drinking-horn, which is applied gold kid. The triangular motifs at the top are cut Vilene shapes, painted and stuck to the background. For other figures from the Isle of Lewis chess set, see pages 126–127.

A BRIEF HISTORIC SURVEY

An understanding of a country's history is by no means essential to an appreciation of its artistic styles but I have found that it helps to know something of the conditions under which they flourished, what was there to start with, and how they developed alongside the cultures of neighbouring countries.

Simultaneous development is a phenomenon that occurs when the same thing, perhaps a motif or a technique, appears more or less simultaneously hundreds or even thousands of miles apart for no apparent reason. Historians often explain this by the migration of people who introduce new ideas as they re-settle, and although this certainly did happen, it doesn't allow for the fact that good ideas can occur to more than one person (or society) at one time. Embroiderers know as well as anyone that it can, and does. They also know how much we rely on the lending, borrowing and adapting of designs, styles and methods and how we use them to suit our needs even when the origin of the idea has been lost in history.

This is what happened with the Celts, the Anglo-Saxons and the Vikings: designs appeared simultaneously across Europe with the distinct Celtic stamp upon them; others were absorbed, re-invented and adapted to whatever level of skill was there, to the materials available, and to the requirements and influences of society. To take one example: as the various kingdoms of seventh-century Britain began once again to embrace Christianity, contact with Rome was established which allowed access to those places where silk was bought and sold. As silk fabric and threads became more available, so did the standard of fine needlework soar in those places where time and conditions were right: noble houses and convents. No wonder, then, that those to benefit most from this astonishing development were the royalty and ecclesiastics who needed it and could afford to pay for the gold and gems that adorned it. They had the workforce too. The designs utilised by these expert embroiderers were very similar to those used by the goldsmiths, sculptors and calligraphers of the time. Everyone borrowed and adapted. Patterns were taken from the expensive silk textiles of faraway Byzantium. It showed you were up-to-date.

But it was not an era of individual 'names' as our society is today. Then, it was safer and more acceptable to conform, to follow the trends. One could excel, and many did, but except in a few rare cases, it is not the craftsman's name that is recorded but that of the donor. This is not to say that the hand of every brilliant individual has been lost amongst all the artefacts that survive. In calligraphy, especially, and in metalwork too, works can be recognised as belonging to one craftsman. In embroidery, where the women tended to be of the noble or royal estate, we are given a few names as well as one particular designer, St Dunstan. However, these are rare exceptions.

This is by no means a scholarly treatise on early English needlework; rather it is what I have discovered about embroidery in particular, which has brought me a little closer to those wonderful women who worked in such difficult and dangerous times yet who still managed to produce masterpieces of such an exceptionally high standard. What follows is a brief overview of those unsettled times. It is important to remember, though, that all these named periods in England's history, Iron Age, Celtic, Anglo-Saxon and Viking, overlap each other sometimes by a hundred years or more. Every history book gives slightly different dates, according to the latest thinking.

THE CELTS

This was never the name of a particular nation or tribe, nor was the term 'Celt' ever applied by ancient writers to the people of the British Isles or Ireland. At best, it describes a society and culture occupying territories throughout Europe from the fifth century B.C. onwards, which both adapted to and influenced the economy, society and culture of the countries in which they settled. From the third century B.C.,

St Dunstan (see page 32).

the unique artistic achievements of Celtic-speaking people from Switzerland were brought to Britain, particularly metalworking in gold and bronze, and later the complex art of illuminated calligraphy.

Celtic influence continued to survive in those parts of the British Isles remaining outside the authority of Rome, chiefly on the outer edges, Wales, Cornwall, Scotland and Ireland, which is why, after the Roman withdrawal in A.D. 409, the Celtic-speaking communities and their art styles were still intact. It is from the Celts that the interlaced strapwork designs originate, the multiple spiral patterns, and the beautiful lettering of the earliest manuscripts.

Textiles from the Bronze Age (c. 2000–500 B.C.) and from the Iron Age (c. 750–150 B.C.) have survived in fragments mainly from peat bogs and burials, revealing that weaving skills and added stitchery were even then well developed. These ancient societies, living in round huts of wood, mud, thatch and stone in hill-top fortifications, were not only well and warmly dressed but richly ornamented with solid gold jewellery of the most intricate workmanship. No doubt their garments were equally well ornamented. In early Britain (we were not known as England until hundreds of years later), woven plaids, fringes and tassels appear to have been a favourite decoration on textiles, but in Denmark entire costumes dating from the Bronze Age have been well preserved in the peat bogs of the Jutland peninsula. In one case, the woollen jacket of a lady buried in an oak coffin shows a geometric pattern of embroidery on the sleeve.

The Anglo-Saxons

The Roman invasion of Britain came in two waves; the first short one in 55 B.C.; the second, in A.D. 43, lasted some three hundred and sixty years. In some respects, the Romanised Britons and Celts who remained after the Roman departure (A.D. 409) wished they had not left so hurriedly, for Britain was already being invaded from all sides by barbarians from north-west Germany (known as Saxons), by Angles from Denmark, by Jutes from Jutland, by Norwegians and Swedes too. By the seventh century A.D., these barbarians had settled for good, Britain became known as Engle-land, and the language was further expanded from the Celtic and Latin (the Roman influence) to Germanic and Scandinavian. Latin and Old English were the written languages, but people spoke whatever they knew best. However, Anglo-Saxons began at this time to keep written records of what was happening, and so it is from this period that we learn more about the textiles and embroidery being sent as gifts, about the high standards achieved, and about the costumes being worn by those important enough to be depicted on manuscripts.

Morwenna's tasselled sleeve

I imagined Morwenna to be a typical Cornish girl, dark-haired and fond of deep reds and gold. She would have been a skilled embroiderer too, good at making tassels and patterns like those on carved stone Celtic monuments. This panel is mostly on silk using stitches known in the tenth century.
Courtesy of Susan H. Evans

Even so, few actual examples of Anglo-Saxon embroidery have survived the centuries. Natural fibres degrade quickly in damp soil and sometimes only imprints of textiles on metal grave-goods remain to tell archaeologists what was once there. Other factors have contributed to their disappearance too. When garments were made by such time-consuming processes, they were passed down from mother to daughter, or bequeathed in wills, until they had literally fallen to pieces. After that, rags were used for all kinds of purposes, even to bung holes in boats. Very little remains. Those special garments heavy with gold thread would have been stolen and stripped of their bullion by raiders, Viking and Norman, and melted down for coinage, the fabric chopped up and re-used, just as it was during the Dissolution of the Monasteries hundreds of years later (1536–40).

Fortunately, there are still a few examples of Anglo-Saxon embroidery in existence for us to see at first hand in England, Belgium and France. In the treasury crypt of Durham Cathedral, open to the public, are some of the exquisite vestments found in the tomb of St Cuthbert, the great seventh-century Northumbrian Bishop of Lindisfarne. The embroideries were executed in Winchester in the early tenth century and represent some of the finest goldwork ever made, even by today's standards.

At Maaseik, in Belgium, there is an embroidery dating from c. 800 which belonged to the Convent of Sts Harlindis and Relindis at Aldeneik. The silk-on-linen embroidery outlined in gold thread is of Anglo-Saxon workmanship and is quite different in style, quality and technique from the St Cuthbert vestments, which may partly be due to the fluidity of traditions at this time.

Celtic, Anglo-Saxon and Viking women

Costumes differed considerably from one era to another and from place to place, whether in England, Scotland, Ireland or Scandinavia. This painting shows women's clothes of the tenth and eleventh centuries when English women did not, apparently, have anything hanging from their belts except a purse. Since artwork produced at this time is often ambiguous and difficult to interpret, experts still disagree about the rules concerning things like head-coverings and fastenings, for instance, and about where brooches were worn.

This fluidity is perfectly demonstrated by the Bayeux Tapestry, actually an embroidery made by Anglo-Saxon women in the years following the Battle of Hastings in 1066. Now housed in the town of Bayeux, Normandy, it is worked in fine wool on linen, and is a narrative meant to be read as one walks around the walls of a great Norman hall. It is an incredible 70 metres (approximately 77 yards) long.

The most outstanding fact regarding Anglo-Saxon embroidery is that its fame spread far and wide throughout Christendom and was unsurpassed in execution and style by any other country. The quotations found scattered throughout this book will attest to its perfection and value. And if you need further convincing, try to see the Durham vestments for yourself. They are small, dimly lit and delicate, but the scale and execution of the goldwork defy belief.

The Vikings

From the mid-700s onwards, Anglo-Saxon records are scattered with accounts of the pagan Viking raids that took place all round our poorly protected coastline, even as far as Ireland and the northernmost tips of Scotland, taking everything of value, even the people themselves. The Vikings were skilled sailors from Norway, Sweden and Denmark, fearsome warriors, and they intended to stay. It makes a long and bitter story but, by 1016, England was ruled by its first Danish king, Cnut. He cemented the alliance by marrying the widow of the man he'd conquered (Aethelred), and although this probably made little difference to the lives of ordinary folk except in terms of recovery, it marked yet another stage in the power struggles of the Anglo-Saxon/Scandinavian heirarchy.

But it also marks a period when the Danish Ringerike style of ornament was introduced into southern England, which apparently blended seamlessly with the English 'Winchester style' of manuscript decoration. In northern England, sculptors in stone were more influenced by the 'Borre' and 'Jellinge' styles of Viking art as a result of which York became an important centre of stone-carving. In other parts, metalworkers adopted the later 'Urnes' style, resulting in a distinctive tenth-century art best described as Anglo-Scandinavian.

Regarding embroidery, it is difficult to assess the impact of Scandinavian styles on so little existing evidence, though it is highly likely that changes took place as they did in most other arts and crafts. Quite possibly there were changes in weaving processes too, and certainly the Viking women had techniques in netting, knotting and the use of metal threads that remained peculiar to them.

Who embroidered, and what?

Given the extreme macho-culture of the Celts, Anglo-Saxons and Vikings, and the apparently strict segregation of women's work from men's, it is almost inconceivable that any man, not even a monk, would have embroidered. They would wear it, yes, and design it too, but the actual work would have been left to the women until, in the thirteenth century, it became a profession worthy of male involvement. This later period in the history of embroidery is known as Opus Anglicanum, and was built on the traditions and techniques of the Anglo-Saxon embroiderers.

The women with both time and wealth to embroider were not from the lower (serf) class but noblewomen, their slaves and servants, and royalty. According to Domesday, there were some who took in pupils in return for payment. Nunneries in particular included fine needlework in their daily routine, and it was in these holy places that church vestments would have been made. Widows of noble birth usually ended their days in nunneries, and embroidery would have been a favourite occupation befitting their status.

No doubt more lowly householders would have found a few spare moments to work a line or two of chain or stem stitch round a neckline or sleeve, but the basic conditions in which the majority of people lived would have made it impossible to replicate the finer work of their superiors. Nor would it have been economically possible or fitting for a serf to dress beyond his station, though we know that the skills of loom and tablet weaving were an important part of every woman's work, high born or low.

While nuns embroidered chasubles and altar cloths for their bishops, queens adorned their husbands' garments for both ordinary and state occasions.

Queen Edgyth (pronounced Edith) embroidered her husband's gowns with complicated floral designs, and probably her own too. Wall-hangings were as much a part of recording events and extolling men's virtues as the professional harpist/singer (i.e. the *scop*) was in Anglo-Saxon society, as described so vividly in the Old English story of Beowulf. The wife of the Essex chieftain Byrhtnoth was embroidering a beautiful curtain to celebrate his victories when her husband was killed at the Battle of Maldon in 941. She later donated the curtain to the minster at Ely. The designer and patron of the Bayeux Tapestry may even have seen Byrhtnoth's curtain hanging at Ely. Even the daughter of England's first Norman king, William, may have had a gold-embroidered hanging surrounding her bed. The fragmentary Oseberg Tapestry, a true tapestry and therefore just outside the scope of this book, is nevertheless an example of the parallel Viking tradition of decorating walls with narrative embroideries.

In addition to garments and wall-hangings, banners were also embroidered by women for their menfolk, meant to be carried into battle and used as a rallying point. The black Viking raven must have struck fear into many an Englishman's breast, and the Fighting Man of Wessex was the banner to which men rallied during the Battle of Hastings in 1066. Tapering pennants are carried by both English and Norman warriors on the Bayeux Tapestry, embroidered with colourful emblems.

EANSWITHA (c. 802), an embroiderer of Hereford, was granted by Denbert, Bishop of Worcester, the lease of a two-hundred-acre farm for life on condition that she would 'renew and scour, and from time to time add to, the dresses of the priests who served in the cathedral church'.

Celtic Influences

Introduction

Of all the materials that survive for hundreds of years buried in the ground, textiles fare the worst. From those artefacts and fragments that remain, however, experts have built up a picture of how those textiles were produced and from what fibres, how they were dyed, the kind of garments being made and worn and, occasionally, the embroidery on them. Informed conjecture may be one way to describe it, but it has to serve until more evidence is discovered.

With this knowledge, today's embroiderers can go even further, imagining the decoration that could conceivably have been used as well as some that might not. This applies to objects like my Anglo-Saxon needlecase (see page 115), for which there is no evidence whatever but which might possibly have been as indispensible then as it is today. Perhaps if a woman of Celtic Britain were to see the loom-weights, tweezers and thread-reels on these pages she might recognise them. She might turn the needlecase over and over in her hands and say, 'Ah yes, I had one very like this.'

This first Book is one of the simplest to construct, consisting of two stiff cardboard covers measuring 8 x 8in (20cm square) with four eyelet holes punched along one edge. The pages are fractionally smaller and made individually from a variety of light cards or heavy-duty papers, some of which are stuck back-to-back for extra strength. Each page has eyelets punched into the spine edge to take two leather thongs knotted at one end, threaded through the holes and tied together on the front cover. These are then threaded with heavy beads of silver, wood, clay and glass. Handmade beads are ideal for this purpose.

Front cover (top)

The front cover consists of glued papers, loosely woven hessian (burlap) and hand-dyed felt stitched and embellished with acrylic paint, French knots, running stitch and the reverse side of a patterned fabric. Gold- and bronze-painted strips of heat-distorted Tyvek are stuck and stitched, decorated with tiny gold and bronze beads. A gold fibre-pen was used to highlight some areas.

Back cover (bottom)

The back cover is a very stiff craft paper with a crumpled surface that can be purchased in packs of dark-coloured, A4 sheets. Covered with thick almost undiluted acrylic paint using a stiff brush, this takes on a new life and begins to resemble crumpled fabric. I used a gold fibre-pen to touch the bumps down one edge, accentuating the three-dimensional quality of the surface. Cut to the same size as the back cover (card), it was then glued on and held with bulldog clips to dry.

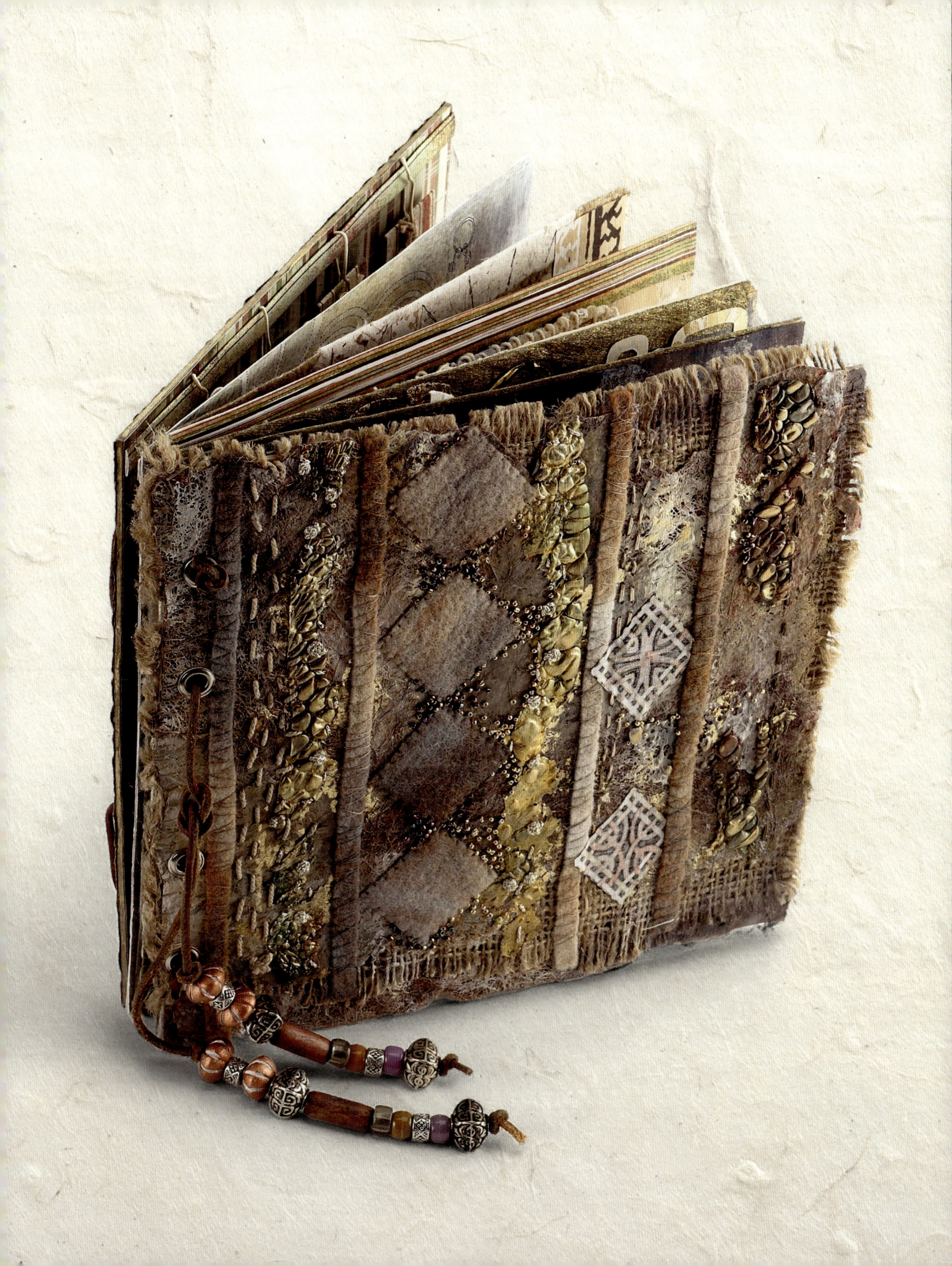
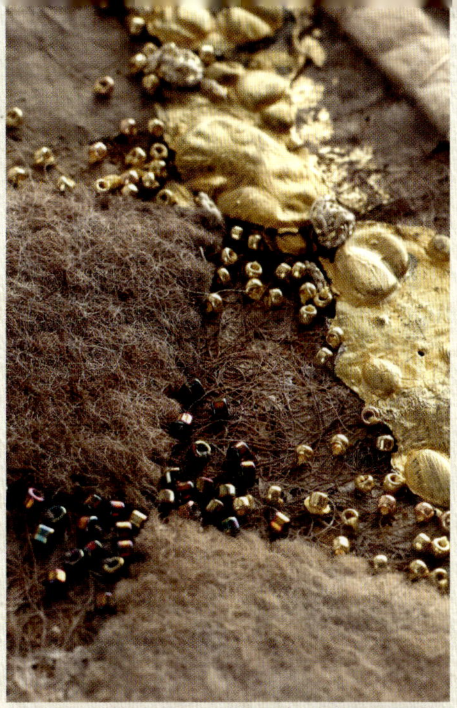
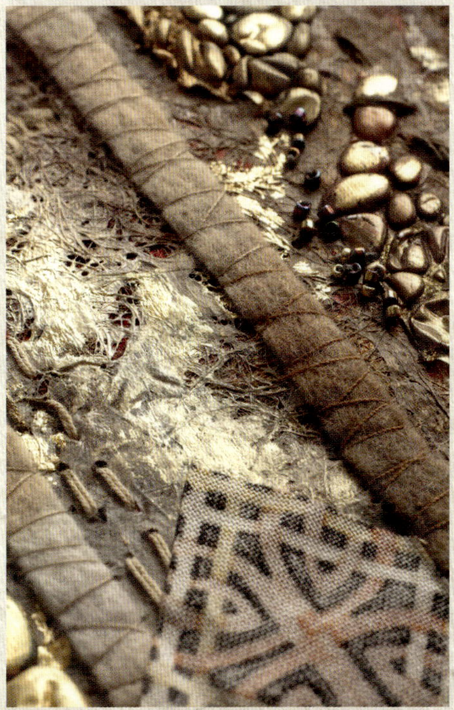
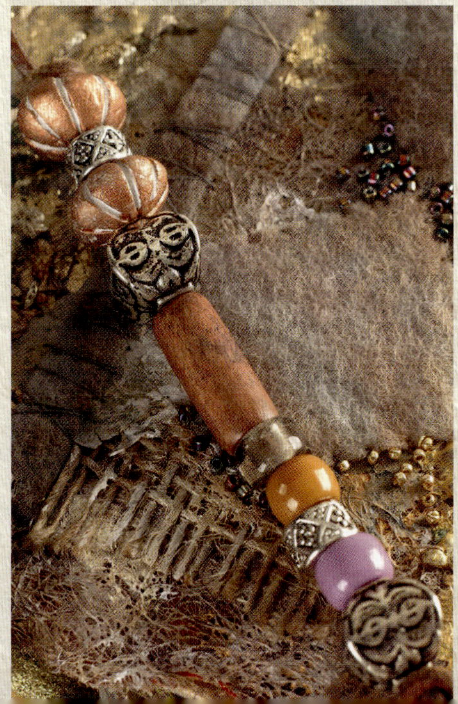

INSIDE FRONT COVER

The twenty-four Runic characters date from c. A.D. 150. Known as the Futhark after the first six (the *th* is counted as one), they were intended to be carved on wood. A later Viking-Age version has sixteen characters, but both versions are known wherever the Vikings settled, except in Iceland and Normandy. Carved on memorials and everyday objects as marks of ownership, they were also used as charms and curses, and for sending messages.

PAGE ONE

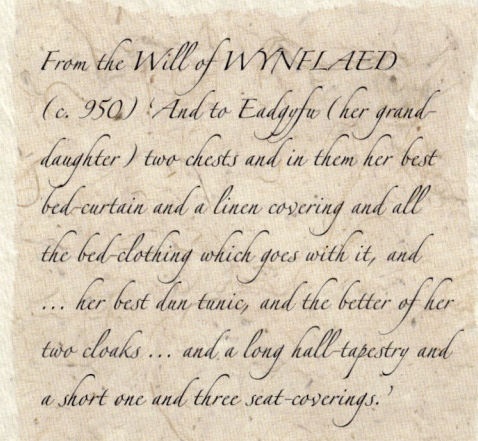

From the Will of WYNFLAED
(c. 950): 'And to Eadgyfu (her grand-
daughter) two chests and in them her best
bed-curtain and a linen covering and all
the bed-clothing which goes with it, and
... her best dun tunic, and the better of her
two cloaks ... and a long hall-tapestry and
a short one and three seat-coverings.'

Page two

Exquisite and complex gold collars (torques) and armbands were made and worn by Celts in all parts of Europe, and these two pages are intended as a celebration of gold ornament together with the natural fibres on which they would have been seen. Perhaps the use of loops and pin tucks would not have been so familiar, but the rows of stitching on the right-hand side are a reconstruction of part of a sleeve found in an early Bronze-Age burial in Denmark. The bead decoration is my own addition, but if the sleeves looked like this, imagine what the rest of the garment was like in the years between 1500 and 500 B.C.

Page three

PAGE FOUR

Needleweaving on a distressed surface of torn paper and scraps of fabric, some stained with tea, creates an impression of an ancient fragment like those found in the Oseberg ship burial in Norway, preserved in unusually good conditions. Here, my use of natural fibres has been extended to cotton which was not available to the Celts or Anglo-Saxons, although used extensively by ancient Egyptians from the third century B.C.

Page Five

Not by any means was all Celtic weaving as rough as this sample implies, though there must have been occasions when shaggy woollen cloaks were needed in cold weather. This sample was constructed on a small cardboard loom wrapped with a string warp, while the weft is a medley of twisted fabrics including unspun wool and silk, muslin, leather, fur and raggy dyed lace.

PAGE SIX

Proof that women used an upright warp-weighted loom as far back as the late seventh century B.C. comes in the form of a bronze pot from Sopron in Hungary, incised with domestic scenes and men hunting. One woman weaves while others play the harp, dance, and spin the thread on a drop spindle.

Page Seven

Through the Saxon arches, we get a glimpse of a woman's tools, some of which would have differed little from those of her Celtic forebears. A workbox made from strips of bone or wood supports two small metal containers thought to be for keeping needles and threads safe, as was the one with the chain. Metal and bone pins are seen below this, not to scale, with a stone loom-weight, a slick-stone of glass or stone used for ironing, a wooden spindle for wool or linen, and a metal pricket on which a beeswax candle is impaled. Candles, rush lights, braziers, fire light and natural light would have been the normal way for women to work. Celtic spiral patterns like those seen in the background would have been familiar to embroiderers, who may have copied them from stone-carvings and metalwork.

25

Page eight

Most dyes for domestic purposes were derived from plants to produce a wide range of colours, though these would vary in intensity according to the type of soil, the climate and the time of year. Leaves, flowers and roots were all used, lichens and tree bark, with or without mordants. While representing the kind of colours obtained from natural sources, those seen here are not all plant-dyed. But every woman would have known where to find the best dyeing plants and how best to dye her wool and linen, whether before or after weaving.

INSIDE BACK COVER

The needlecase

This is covered with a linen, Celtic-patterned printed design cut from a tea-towel. It was first painted with watercolours and acrylics, then outlined with gold paint. I prefer to use ordinary artists' colours, water, gouache or acrylic, rather than specialised fabric paints. They can be used watered down or almost straight from the tube and, unless the embroidery is to be washed, they serve the same purpose with less expense. However, a good range of brushes is essential.

When it was dry and cut to size, I ripped and shredded the fabric to suggest the wear and tear of centuries, then darned the holes over a hand-dyed felt. Heavy-duty (pelmet-weight) Vilene was used to stiffen the cover, scored in two places, lined with a striped cotton to suggest a woody surface, then bits of the patterned tea-dyed tea-towel were applied for pockets and holders.

The gold ring on the front edge is an odd earring and the tie is plaited, and attached to embroidered beaded tassels. The tie wraps around the needlecase to keep it closed.

29

This, I thought, is surely where the Anglo-Saxon woman would have kept her precious tools. Every needle was made by hand; losing one would have been a disaster, for some must have been as fine as ours. Pins with metal and beaded heads are easily duplicated from jewellery 'findings', and from long pins and wooden skewers to represent the bone types. The silver shears are cut from silver card, based on some found in Jorvik (Viking York), as are the tiny tweezers, bone bobbins, and the square bone tablets in the top right-hand pocket used for making decorative bands known as tablet weaving (more about this further on).

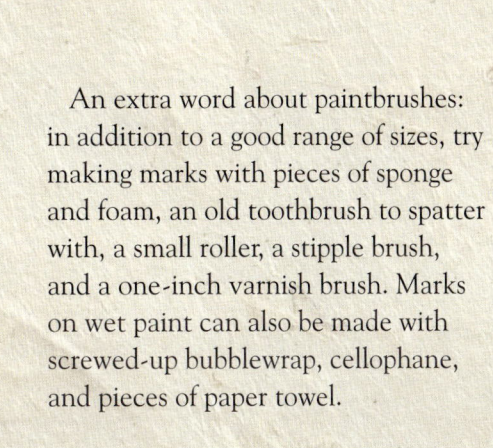

The right-hand flap folds back, revealing fabric samples and the square bone tablets underneath.

No thimbles have been found from this period, so we may assume that these were made of leather which would have decayed completely. Perhaps a block of beeswax might have been kept in the empty pocket, used for waxing threads to prevent tangling. It is quite surprising how little has changed in all the intervening years.

An extra word about paintbrushes: in addition to a good range of sizes, try making marks with pieces of sponge and foam, an old toothbrush to spatter with, a small roller, a stipple brush, and a one-inch varnish brush. Marks on wet paint can also be made with screwed-up bubblewrap, cellophane, and pieces of paper towel.

31

St Dunstan

c. 909—988

Archbishop of Canterbury in 959. Scribe, artist, bellfounder and blacksmith, musician, teacher, royal counsellor, poet and church reformer, educated at the court of King Aethelstan. He designed a stole for a lady-friend to embroider 'with divers sorts of patterns which she would afterwards enrich with gold and gems'.

In this thirteenth-century portrait, St Dunstan wears an embroidered chasuble, a dalmatic with an embroidered hem, a mitre, and his archbishop's pallium, the long end of which can be seen hanging down the front, decorated with purple crosses. He works on a book the cover of which is protected by a white cloth. In his right hand he holds a quill pen; in his left he holds a sharp knife used for erasing unwanted marks from the vellum and for sharpening his quill.

AELFGIFU (or Aelfgyva) of Northampton, first wife of King Cnut (d. 1035), married c. 1013. She was an embroiderer. Altar cloths worked by her were presented by Cnut to the abbeys of Croyland, Cambridgeshire and Romsey, Hampshire.

Wulfwynn, Abbess of Romsey

Wulfwynn was the first of two eleventh-century abbesses who may have been in office during the years of the Norman Conquest and who may even have had a hand in the construction of the Bayeux Tapestry. This is my portrait of her, austere but kindly. Romsey is in Hampshire and boasts one of England's oldest abbeys built on the foundations of the Anglo-Saxon nunnery. As seven out of ten nunneries still in existence at the time of the Conquest were in Wessex (there was no known nunnery in Canterbury at this time), it is more than likely that, organised by Winchester nuns, the Bayeux Tapestry was made in seven different venues under the supervision of seven abbesses.

Leofgyth of Knook

Mentioned in Domesday Book, Leofgyth/Leofgeat held an estate at Knook in Wiltshire, not far away from the nunnery at Wilton which belonged to Queen Edgyth, wife of King Eadward the Confessor. According to Domesday, 'she used to make, and still makes, the embroidery of the king and queen'. This refers to King William and Queen Mathilde, so she was still embroidering after the Conquest. However, she may also have worked on the Bayeux Tapestry, even as a 'consultant'.

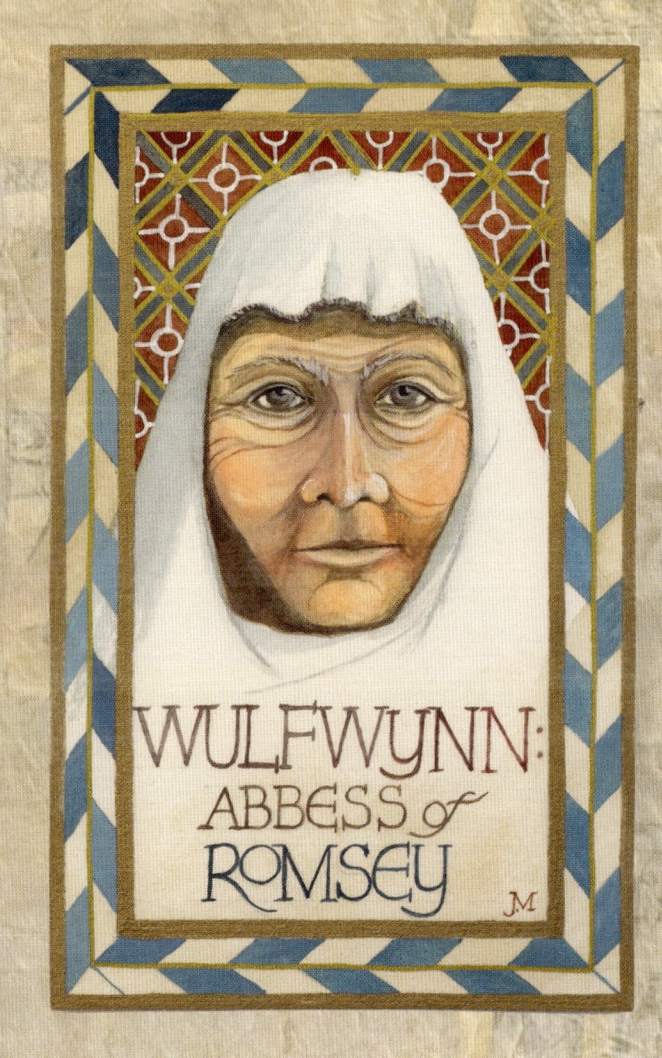

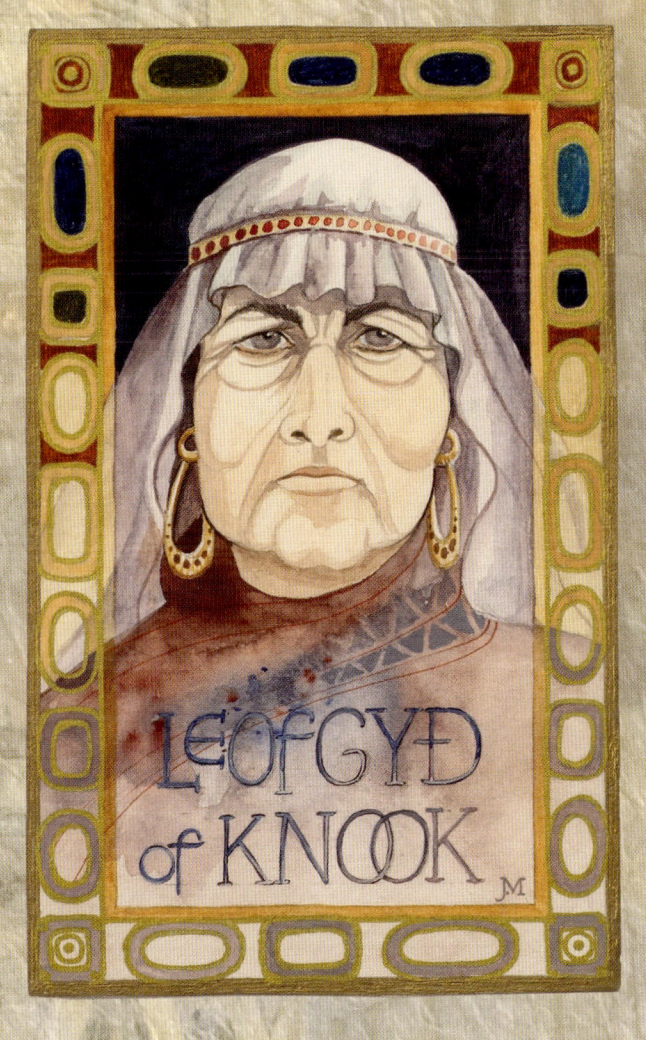

From the Will of WULFWARU (984–1016): 'and I grant to my son Wulfmaer a hall-tapestry and a set of bed-clothes. To Aelfwine my second son I grant a tapestry for a hall and a tapestry for a chamber, together with a table-cover and all the cloths which go with it.'

THE BOOK OF STITCHES

INTRODUCTION

Extensive research has been carried out on ninth- and tenth-century textile fragments found at Jorvik (Viking York) and on finds from London which are supplemented by those from ninth-century Birka in south-east Sweden and tenth-century Hedeby in Denmark. From these investigations, different construction stitches have been identified as well as a variety of ways of using them on wool, linen and silk where, generally speaking, the sewing thread is of the same fibre as the textile on which it is found. But because these textiles were not complete garments, it is often difficult to be sure what item was being stitched.

Several methods of joining fabric were used: overcast on raw and folded edges, rolled edges on silk, running and whip stitches used in a variety of ways. Even the modern run-and-fell seam was common at Jorvik, with variations on Danish finds, and a version of the French seam. Viking needlewomen would often use woollen braids and cords to strengthen and decorate seams, a form of early appliqué; also stem, raised herringbone and chain stitch, all of which are economical with the thread. English embroideries of the same period are remarkably similar in many ways, with the addition of surface couching (of gold threads) and split stitch. Underside couching was not used until a later period. Another type of couching, now known as Bayeux stitch, was worked in wool on linen with outline-stitched shapes.

Other stitches that may have been the forerunners of some known to us today are the Viking loop technique resembling Vandyke stitch, and a kind of knotting known as 'nalebinding', which resembles Ceylon stitch. This nalebinding was used in Bronze-Age Europe as a way of making fabric for socks, mittens and head-coverings. An example of a sock made in this way was found in Jorvik, but there is no evidence that this technique was practised by Anglo-Saxon women. However, I had a pair of socks made for me by a friend, Hazel Uzell, and I can vouch for their warmth, comfort and durability.

Front and back covers

Hand-pieced fabric strips with string-quilted lines over thin wadding, over-painted and stitched with running, buttonhole and feather stitches. The edges of the covers are bound with a Celtic-patterned fabric, over-painted to distress, and fastened with card hinges and gold-painted sticks. The cords are plaited, decorated with beads and more card tabs.

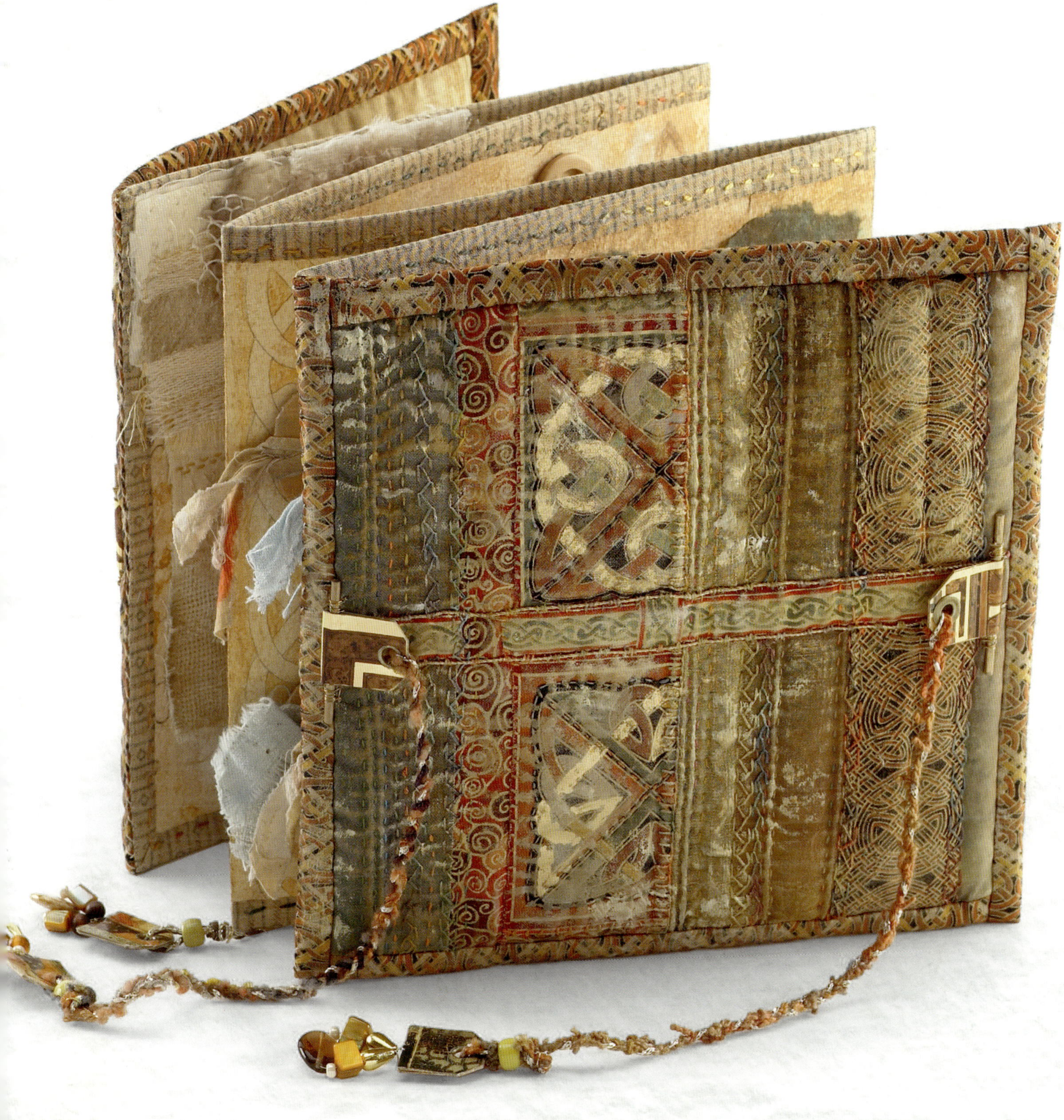
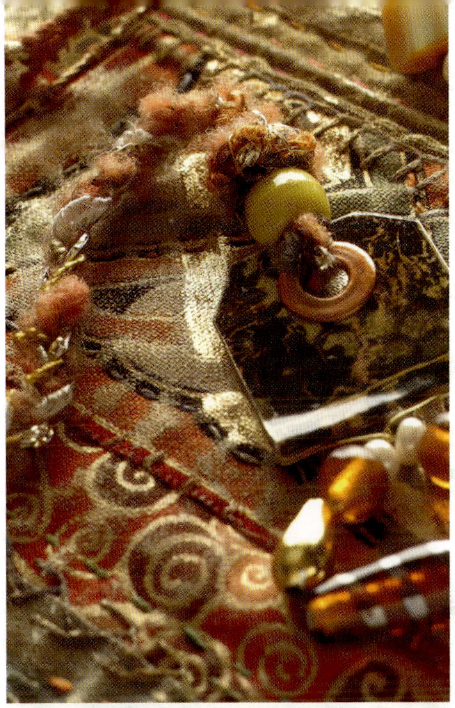
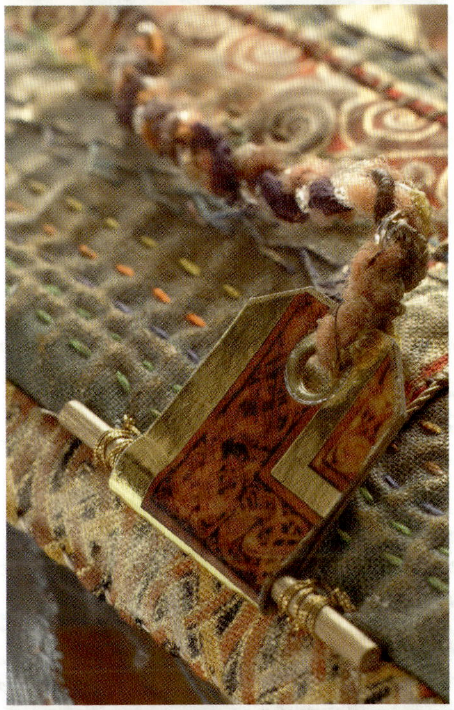
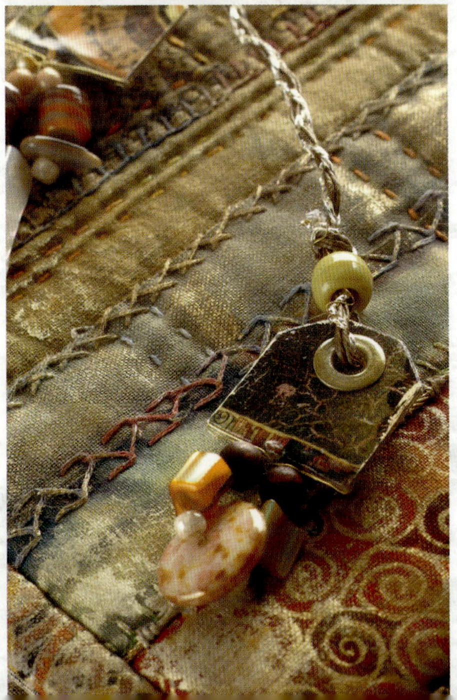

Satin stitch has been identified on a scrap of checked cloth found at Worthy Park in Hampshire, and a late Anglo-Saxon shirt found at Llangors in Wales shows silk embroidery on linen in both plied and unplied threads. Thread-counted stem stitch has been identified, as well as small triangles of buttonhole stitch to reinforce the meeting of several seams. Although this may not have been meant as decoration, it does show that buttonhole stitch was known.

To some of the younger generation, the art of darning may still be a mystery. But when all garments, large and small, were constructed by hand, spun and woven too, darning was an essential task. For this reason, I have included pattern darning in my list of early stitches, as it replicates the tabby weave of handwoven wool when worked on a coarse fabric like canvas or hessian.

From the ninth-century Norwegian burial-ship at Oseberg, the garments of the queen and her attendant were ornamented with appliqué-work in wool, representing animal heads. And at Birka, more appliqué was discovered on the fronts of women's undergarments in the form of tablet-woven bands on a silk background. In another Viking burial at Mammen, a cape was decorated with golden bees, attachments that are now lost but which may have been similar to the Anglo-Saxon find at Prittlewell in England where small gold foil crosses were once attached to a shroud.

Similarly, patches applied over holes, repairs to edges, sewn-on ribbons, braids and strips of decorative fabrics are the forerunners of what we term appliqué, though our methods would not have been seen as an economical use of fabric at that time. In addition, many references are made to the use of jewels, gems, pearls, 'and other precious stones'. One of the royal garments made by Queen Edgyth for her husband is said to have been decorated with little birds and bells. Certainly beads would have been added along hemlines and other edges, as were fringes and tassels.

Fibres and threads

Regarding these early periods of history, it is tempting to think of handspun threads as being coarse and lumpy. Perhaps television costume departments may partly be responsible for that. The truth is that while a certain amount of rough woollen cloth would have been produced for work, linen was far too valuable a fibre to leave to amateurs. Skilled women working on the upright loom produced exceptionally fine fabrics that may have taken months to make. Time consuming, yes, but so was everything else. Apart from home production, there would also have been weaving workshops requiring the skills of dozens of spinners to supply the thread, for it was during the tenth century that more sophisticated horizontal looms were introduced into England, although most homes would still have used the upright loom that leaned against a wall. The linen used for the Bayeux Tapestry, for instance, has a count of fifty-eight threads to the inch, much finer than anything used nowadays for counted-thread techniques. Linen was woven in a variety of patterns that included plain tabby, herringbone, huckaback, lozenge, looped pile, rosette twills and honeycomb.

Silk (Old English *seolc*) was a much rarer fibre in Anglo-Saxon England than either wool or the more time-consuming linen, very little of it being available during the fifth or sixth centuries. In the seventh century, however, as a result of the new wave of Christianity and contact with Rome (where there was no shortage from silk suppliers in Byzantium, the Near East, North Africa and Southern Spain), we have written evidence of silk fabrics being sent to Britain as gifts, bribes and donations. Even so, little of this has been found, perhaps because it and the gold threads woven into it were of value to Viking and Norman raiders and because, as a fine natural fibre, it degrades over many centuries. By the eleventh century, silk was not uncommon in England for by this time there was a network of merchants who traded across the continents, bringing back all kinds of luxury goods, including silk threads for embroidery.

A detail from the embroidery on page 48.

These little sample cards belong to the Book pages on pages 44 and 45.

It was well known throughout Christendom that Anglo-Saxon women excelled in the art of embroidery, especially in the use of gold thread on royal and ecclesiastical vestments. Gold thread was made by beating almost pure gold into wafer-thin sheets before cutting them into narrow strips known as lamella. These were then wound round a core of fibres, either silk or a single horse-hair, or even linen or wool. Gold threads of an incredible fineness were used on the St Cuthbert vestments: one hundred and twelve threads per inch and, on the maniple, one hundred and twenty-eight threads per inch. Experts believe that the gold embroidery was beaten to spread the threads, while those on other pieces appear to have been flattened beforehand. This kind of thread is known as aurum battutum. Silver threads were made in the same way but, as with the gold in archaeological finds, the core will often have rotted away leaving only a spiral of metal behind.

The Viking method of producing gold thread was to draw the metal through a series of holes of decreasing size to make a solid wire which could be used alone or wound round a core of fibres. Both kinds of gold thread were used in weaving braids and bands, particularly in tablet weaving. In England, centres of gold thread production were at Taplow in Buckinghamshire, in Suffolk, the Isle of Wight, and in Kent.

THE BOOK

This is an eight-page accordian, or zig-zag, book with embroidered covers and fabric-bound edges. The pages are made of heavy watercolour paper scored lightly along the folds, painted and decorated. Heavy-duty (pelmet-weight) Vilene was sandwiched between each of the two covers for extra strength.

At the Ecclesiastical Council of 747 at CLOFESHOH, a place which has not yet been identified, English nuns were exhorted to devote more attention to the reading of books and the singing of psalms than to their needlework.

INNER PANELS

38

39

OUTER PANELS

41

INSIDE FRONT COVER

Although it is unlikely that shapes would have been cut out and applied, as this one is, appliqué was known in the form of braids and strips meant to decorate seams and to disguise raw edges. The building is taken from the church at Bosham on the Bayeux Tapestry, cut out of handmade paper and stitched to cotton with a thin padding beneath.

Page One

Simple stitches known to Anglo-Saxon women. Top left: split stitch; top right: outline stitch on the left, stem stitch on the right; bottom left: chain stitch; bottom right: buttonhole stitch. Each patch is bordered by running stitch.

PAGE TWO

Little pouches and shaped cards make an interesting display of stitches and/or techniques against a background of painted watercolour paper. Each pouch hangs from a bone ring and is ornamented with a tassel using jewellery 'findings', gold kid and beads, and each sample is meant to complement the lining pattern of its own pouch.

From the left: spirals of stem, running and whipped running stitch; more running stitch worked over torn strips of painted fabric; couching, textured yarns, metal foil and wood; simple pattern-darning over hessian (burlap).

44

PAGE THREE

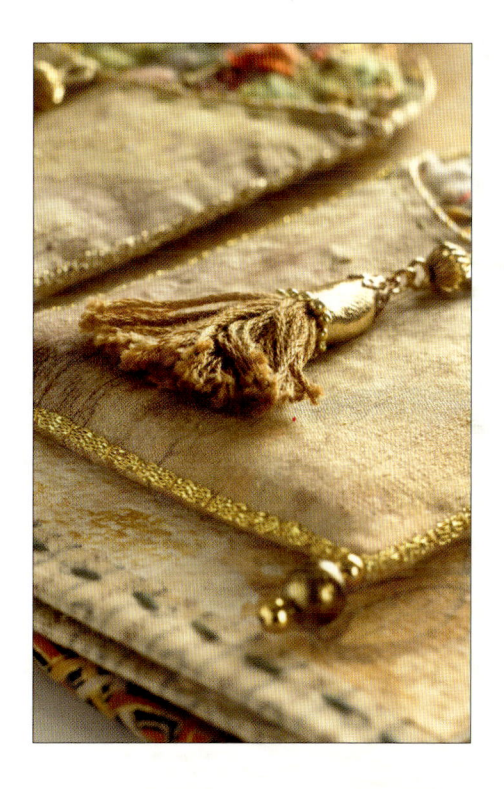

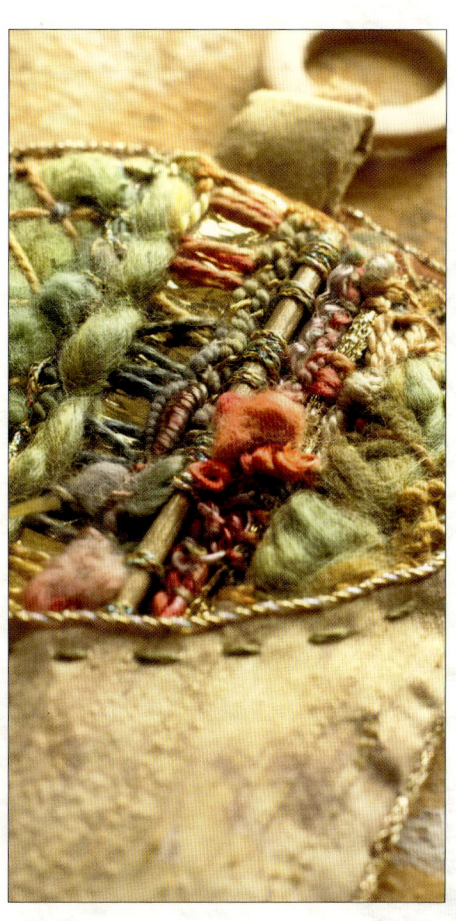

45

PAGE FOUR

Count Guy of Ponthieu is seen on the Bayeux Tapestry wearing a padded gambeson in a pattern of shingles. For some reason, the embroiderer chose to fill the shapes with colour instead of leaving it plain, as it would have been, thereby giving an impression of patchwork which has puzzled historians ever since. In fact, it is quilting.

COUNT GUY OF PONTHIEU FROM THE BAYEUX TAPESTRY

INSIDE BACK COVER

The quilted gambeson was worn beneath, and sometimes over, chain mail to afford extra protection. Quilting was used decoratively, as can be seen in three instances on the Bayeux Tapestry, and this design is taken from a brooch known as the Ripon Jewel, dating from the seventh century.

47

PAGE FIVE

Needlelace stitches resemble the Viking technique known as nalebinding, a dense stitch used for making socks. This sample of Ceylon stitch is intended to look like a fragment from those times, although Ceylon stitch is now also used in needlelace.

48

Page six
stitch diagrams

Top row: running stitch and whipped running stitch; second row: buttonhole, chain and split stitch; third row: herringbone, couching and feather stitch; fourth row: Ceylon stitch, and the last seam on page eight. The first seam of running stitches passes through all three layers.

PAGE SEVEN
SEAMS AND HEMS

These pages show only a few of the methods known to the Anglo-Saxon Scandinavian women, and most of these are very much in use today, one way or another. The samples are mounted on card 'labels', the ends of which are decorated with bought craft papers and rags.

A: from the top, a strip of red silk is sewn over a running-stitch seam to enclose the raw edges. The one below this shows a similar effect using a woven tape. The bottom seam shows a raw edge of fabric oversewn to the one below.

B: from the top, these are hems showing two rows of running stitch over a single fold of fabric; herringbone stitch over a single fold; hemstitch over a double fold; overcast stitch over a folded edge which may be either single or double.

50

Page eight

C: the top seam has both raw edges laid together and joined by a running stitch from the reverse side. This makes a very neat seam. The seam below this has two folded edges laid together, edge to edge, connected by a small overcast stitch. The raw edges are left on the reverse side.

D: the top seam has both raw edges turned down and held in place by a running stitch that does not show, then held together with overcast stitch. A diagram of this can be seen at the bottom of page six.

THE BAYEUX STITCH BOOK

INTRODUCTION

The Book is based on a purchased spiral-bound volume with hard covers and brown pages. By removing the metal spiral, it is possible to take out many of the pages, to work on them separately, to change the order of them, and to regulate the thickness of the finished Book. When all this is done, there are all kinds of fastenings that can be used, but I found hinged metal rings to be most convenient, especially as the silver circles echoed the pattern of windows on the front cover. To decorate, I hung a narrow leather thong from each ring and threaded it with chunky bone and silver beads, wrapping the ends with a self-adhesive metallic foil strip.

Bayeux stitch was first identified as the laidwork filling used on the tapestry which, although belonging to Normandy, was made in England by Anglo-Saxon women in the years just after the Norman invasion of 1066. As with other forms of laidwork (i.e. couched fillings), most of the thread is seen on the surface of the fabric, an economy of importance at this time when the making of threads was labour intensive.

Since those early times when it was used to fill in shapes, more adventurous ideas and more variety of threads and fabrics have extended the scope of this versatile stitch. Originally worked in the same thread for each of the three elements (see page 58), the samples shown here are just a few of the effects that can be achieved when those elements are prised apart. The use of a frame to hold the fabric taut is optional, but I always find it easier to use one.

Front cover (top)

The front of the Book was covered with a layer of heavy-duty Vilene painted with acrylics and pierced with six circular windows under which are placed samples of Bayeux stitch in different colourways. The removed circles were shaped into Celtic crosses, and the circles cut from those were also added to the design.

Back cover (bottom)

Two windows reconstructed from fragments of coloured glass can be seen in the Anglo-Saxon Church of St Paul at Jarrow in Northumbria. Divided as they are into small sections, the designs are ideal for Bayeux stitch.

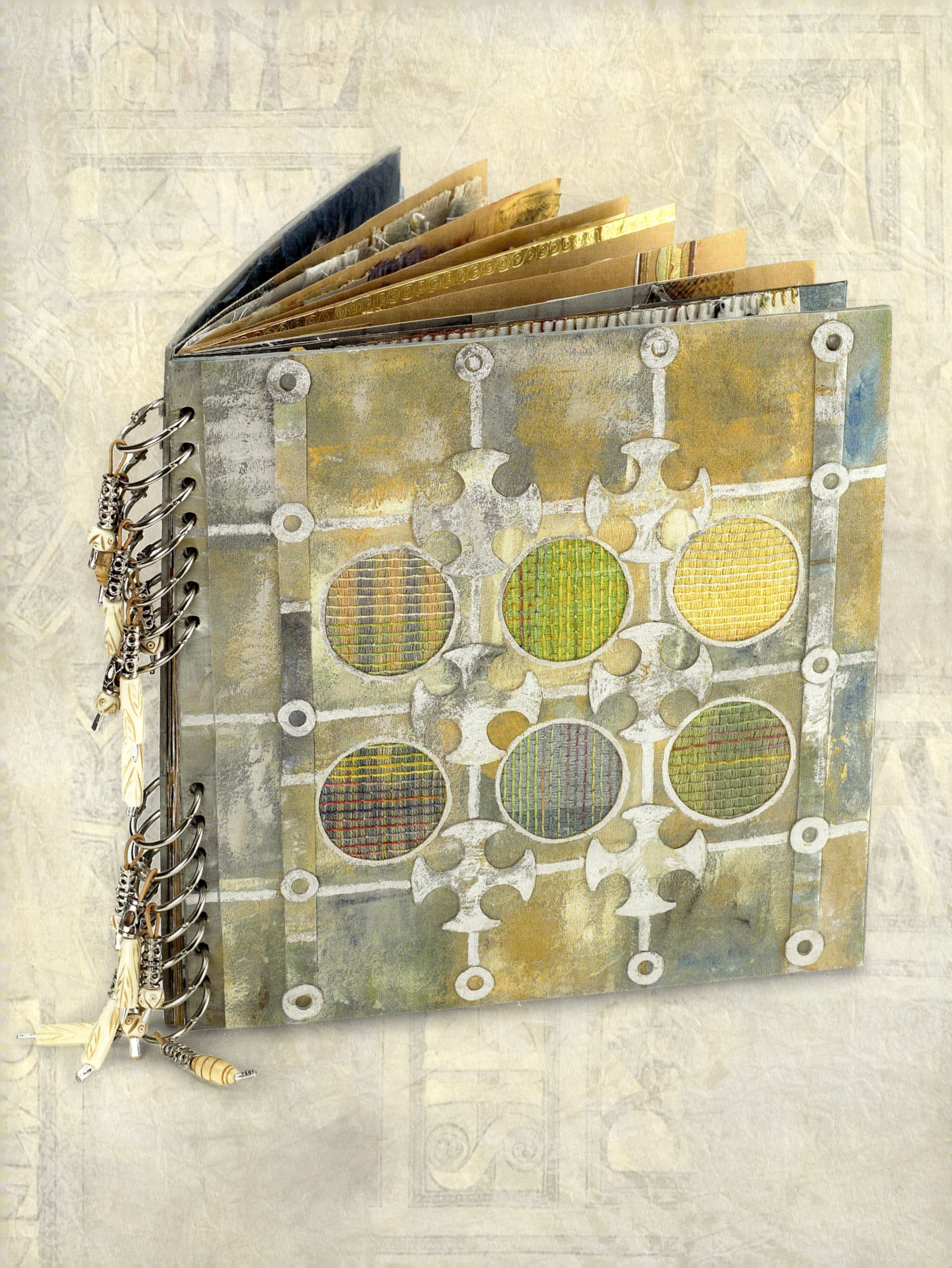
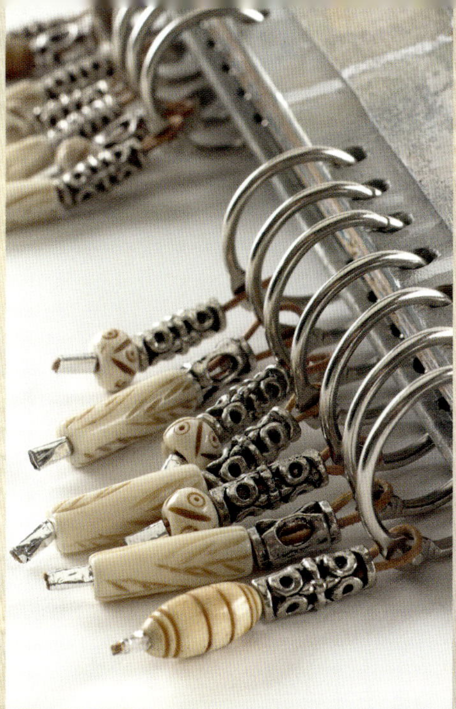
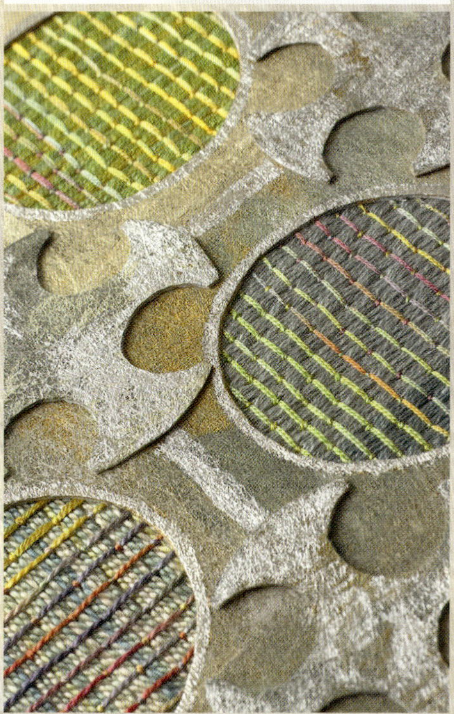
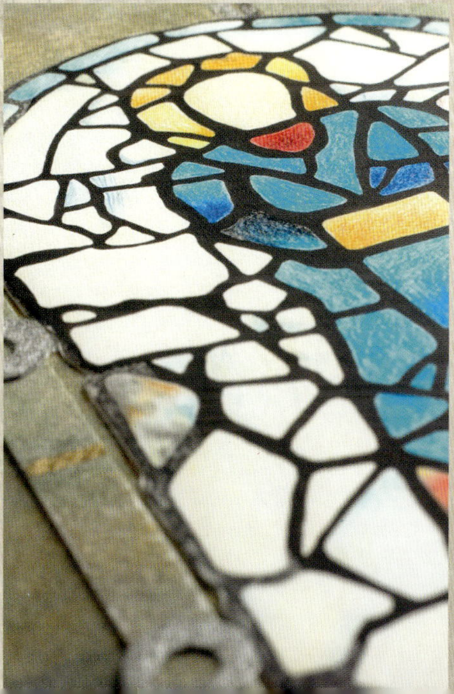

INSIDE FRONT COVER

This design is from an eleventh-century tile belonging to St Mary's Abbey in Winchester, formerly the Anglo-Saxon Nunnaminster which is where I believe the Bayeux Tapestry to have been conceived and partly made. Unlike the original method of working, I have made use of stranded cottons of different combinations to suggest light and shade.
Private collection.

Page One

The original 'tapestry', actually an embroidery, is worked in two-ply worsted yarns on a very fine linen, as seen in this sample which follows exactly the same direction of stitches made by the embroiderer. The outline would have been worked first to establish the charcoal lines before they rubbed off, filling in all the tiny spaces afterwards. This is probably not the way we would proceed nowadays when sometimes we may choose to omit the outline stitch altogether. The yarns used on this sample are plant-dyed, which accounts for the subtle variation of colour.

PAGE TWO

Saxon arches of creamy-white stone outline the entrances and windows to the Church of St Lawrence at Bradford-on-Avon in Wiltshire. On a background of patterned fabrics meant to represent overgrown ruins, this sample is worked in many neutral shades in all directions, with variegated threads to outline the stones. Irregular buttonhole stitch blends the background patterns together. Dating from the tenth century, St Lawrence's is one of the best-known Anglo-Saxon churches still in existence.
Photographs by Glennis Walton

56

Page three

KING WIGLAF OF MERCIA (c. 833) gave a cloak embroidered with the Battle of Troy to Croyland Abbey.

57

Page four

Bayeux stitch is composed of three elements:

1. The laid threads cover the shape from side to side. These resemble satin stitches on the right side, but instead of passing across the reverse side, as satin stitch does, the thread is brought up to the surface next to where it went down. This is why it is easier to work on a fine linen rather than a coarse one, the alternative being to back the fabric with a soft fine calico and stitch through both pieces together.

2. A top thread is placed across the laid threads at intervals but, if the same thread is being used for the next element too (i.e. the holding stitch), this will be worked as each top thread is laid, taking you back to the same side each time.

3. The holding stitch pegs each top thread down and is essentially a stab stitch made with a vertical needle.

As can be seen from the sample, the shapes and stitches can be made in all directions with a different coloured thread for each element. Random-dyed/variegated threads are particularly useful. The use of outline or stem stitch is optional, depending on the design.

Page five

A more formal pattern known as the 'Pelta' or 'Little Shield' is first drawn on to the plain background fabric before being filled in with Bayeux stitch in two directions with no outline stitch. This pattern was well known in Anglo-Saxon England. A selection of purchased craft papers decorates these pages, some cut into Celtic knotwork borders.

59

PAGE SIX

There are three methods of working curves in Bayeux stitch. The one on the left follows the shape with vertical and horizontal lines, while the one on the right is worked in wedge-shaped blocks, as seen at the lower bend. The joins between these blocks are hidden in every case by the top threads and holding stitches, giving the impression of a continuous curve. The centre diagram shows how the curve can be entirely filled in with long and short stitches (and/or split stitch) before being crossed by lines of top threads and holding stitches. Packed closely together, the laid threads will blend and follow even the tightest curve.

The stitch diagrams at the bottom of the page show outline stitch on the left, where the thread is held to the left of the needle, and stem stitch on the right, where the thread falls on the right. Use whichever stitch replicates the twist of the thread you are using, as this will produce a smoother line, especially on curves. For very tight curves, I always prefer to use a split stitch, sometimes held in place by a stab stitch.

Page seven

A simple exercise in colour changes shows how, by the use of different top threads and holding stitches, the colour beneath can undergo a subtle shift in tone.

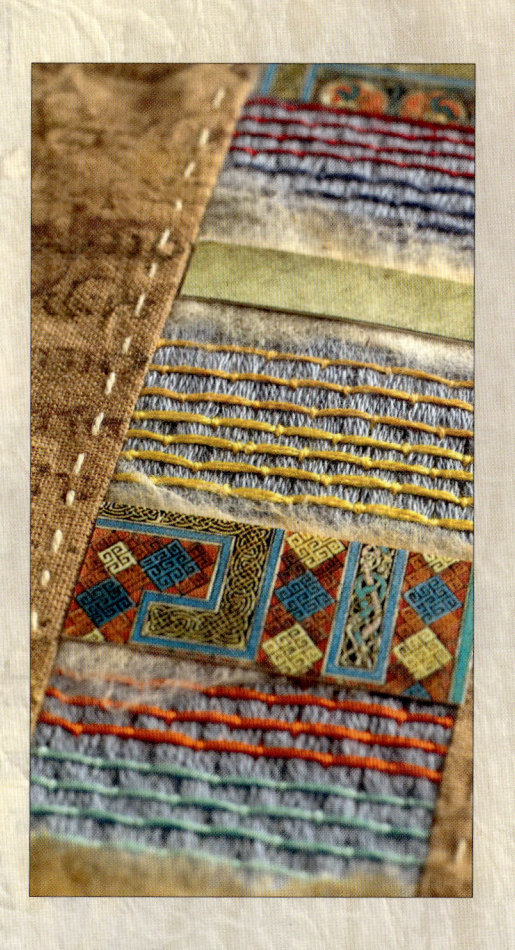

PAGE EIGHT
THE FIELD CUSHION

There was no standard measurement for area or distance in Anglo-Saxon England. Travel was on foot or by horseback, the distance being the time it took for the journey. Land was measurable in terms of how much of it could be ploughed by a team of oxen, how many sheep and cattle it could sustain, or how many people could live there. Plough-land was divided into strips so that one villager did not hold all the best bits while another held the worst. Each part of the country had its own words for land, some of which are listed here and a few embroidered round the borders of my cushion, now in a private collection.

Page nine

A collage of painted paper, card and photographs is one way of composing an impression of tones, directions, patterns and textures which, if viewed from a distance, looks very like an aerial photograph.

63

Page ten

Two important ship burials, one at Sutton Hoo in Essex from the seventh century, and the other at Oseberg in Norway from the ninth century, illustrate the outstanding skills of metalworkers in those times. The handle-mount of a wooden bucket is decorated with this tiny figure bearing a square plaque which, although discovered in Norway, was most likely made by Celtic craftsmen in Ireland. The Sutton Hoo treasure, much of which may be seen in the British Museum, shows masterpieces of minute enamelling techniques decorating clasps, buckles and sword pommels. Some of the patterns are shown here.

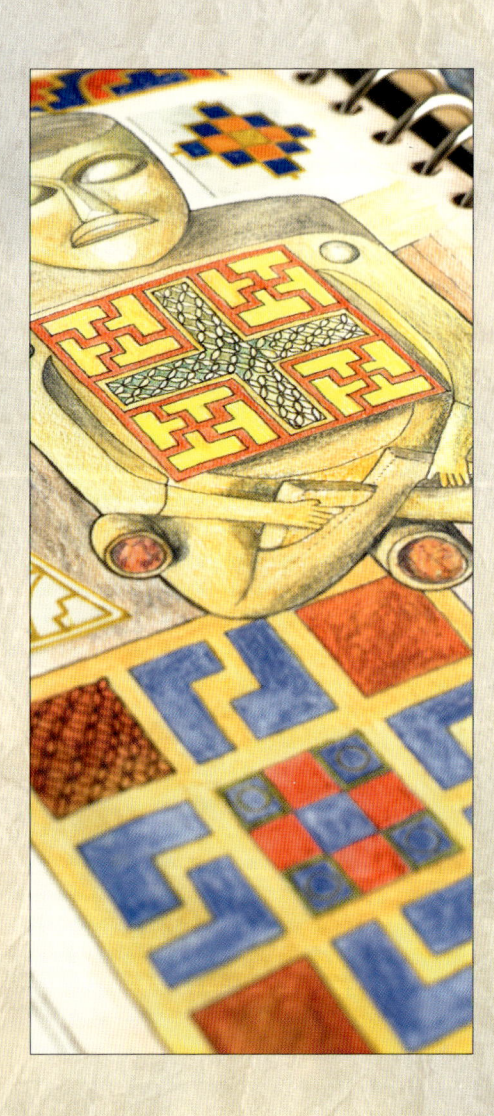

64

Page eleven

A paper, card and fabric collage with paint is one way of discovering how colour can be arranged for a panel in Bayeux stitch, avoiding the too-precise look of hard edges.

Page twelve

Bayeux stitch experiments with a couched first layer instead of the usual laid threads.

Top left: kebab sticks wrapped with tubular knitting ribbon couched down with a top thread held down by beads. Half of the sample is couched with a textured yarn.

Top right: gold self-adhesive ribbon couched with lines of textured knitting wool and bead chips.

Bottom left: textured knitting yarn couched with stranded cotton and beads.

Bottom right: unspun cotton waste spread on to the background held down by a random-dyed silk and the same holding stitch. Over this, two layers of herringbone stitch are worked, one in a fine gold thread.

Page thirteen

Torn strips of fabric are twisted and laid for the first element of Bayeux stitch, couched down with an invisible stitch. The second element is thick string couched with cotton thread, then whipped loosely with a textured knitting yarn.

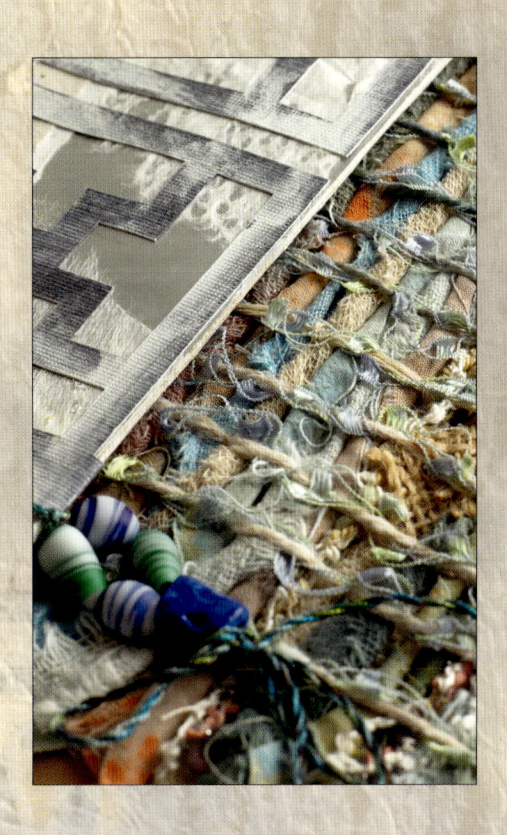

67

Page fourteen

Bayeux stitch can also be worked on canvas using any thread that will pass through the holes. Textured yarns can be couched down instead, and occasional tent stitches will fill in any uncovered spaces.

Inside back cover

Near the Anglo-Saxon Church of St Paul at Jarrow, Northumbria, small pieces of coloured glass were found at the on-site glass workshop, some of the first ever to be made in England. These have now been re-assembled and placed in the ancient stone church where once the Venerable Bede would have worshipped in the seventh century. These windows make an ideal subject for Bayeux stitch. Two more of these windows can be seen on the back cover of this Book (see page 52).

69

The Bayeux Tapestry box

The idea for this piece came from the box itself which seemed to call for something three-dimensional, and also from the subject on which I was engrossed in the late 1990s, the Bayeux Tapestry. Figures of the patron, the designer and the embroiderers would fit the space perfectly, I thought.

Measuring 12½ x 10 x 4½in (32 x 25.5 x 11.5cm), the front of the box is a patchwork of silk and cotton squares with diagonal squares of Bayeux stitch worked over the corners. Random-dyed and gold threads and changes of direction add interest, with satin stitch and appliqué quatrefoils to fill the spaces. The gold-painted border is cut from card.

The reverse side of the box is also based on patchwork squares, some of which are covered with stitches. The interlaced animal motif and border were cut from card, painted gold, and stuck in place.

Note: when painting a shape cut from card, remember to paint the cut white edges too. This can be done easily with a gold- or matching-coloured fibre-pen.

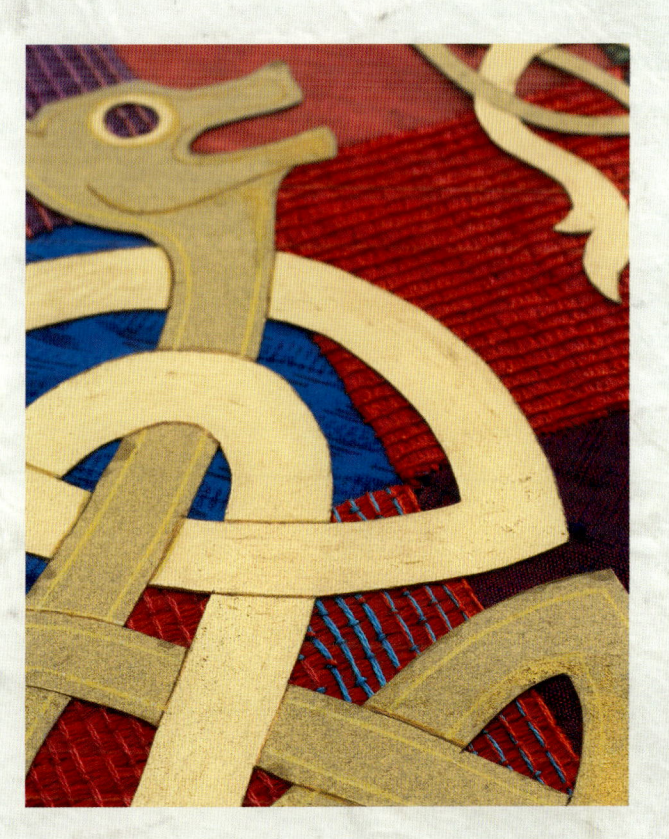

AELFFLAED, widow of the chieftain BYRHTNOTH, hero of the Battle of Maldon in Essex in 991, donated to the Minster of Ely: 'She gave to this church a curtain woven and depicted with the deeds of her husband as a memorial to his virtue.'

The inside space is occupied by five figures set against embroidered panels. On the left are two of the Anglo-Saxon noblewomen who helped to embroider the tapestry in the years immediately after 1066, one of them carrying the woollen yarns used on the project. The appliquéd abbess in the background indicates that their workroom would have been in a nunnery, where many widowed noblewomen would have fled during the years of the Conquest.

The other side is occupied by the monk designer who carries the rolls of drawings, and the man who commissioned the project, the powerful and wealthy Bishop Odo of Bayeux.

The bodies were constructed on a basic shape of heavy-duty Vilene to hold the costume fabrics and padding. The faces, hands and feet were made from painted modelling clay and, as the heads are flat at the back, these were easy to stick to the background. The hands were made with arm extensions, making it easier to insert them into sleeves and bind them in place. The ladies are footless and legless, but the monk has feet and leather sandals.

73

The Dressing-up Book

Introduction

Although it is unlikely that the Anglo-Saxons employed specialist dressmakers, or that anyone would have kept a notebook anything like this one, I have made a fanciful excursion into embroidery with a wearable theme. As an embroiderer, I have responded to the costume of the times without paying too much attention to the exact period, the details of which vary enormously from place to place. Those looking for help with re-enactment costume would do better to consult books dealing with the more precise periods of history.

This Book contains two signatures of pages, each one sewn to a strip of strong paper folded into a 'W' measuring the same height as the pages but only 4in (10cm) wide. When folded lengthwise, twice, each arm of the 'W' will be 1in (2.5cm) wide, and the signatures are sewn into the grooves of the 'W' to connect them. Double-width endpapers were folded in half and glued to the first and last arms of the 'W', and to the inside front and back covers to hold the pages in place.

An embroidered front and back cover of felt reverse-appliqué was prepared all-in-one-piece to fit around a square window cut in the card stiffening. A small painting was stuck in place, its reverse side being covered by the first endpaper. The fastening is made up of four open tubes of felt sewn to the edges of the front and back covers. This can be seen more clearly on page 91. Painted wooden rods were inserted into these tubes, with a space in the centre, to hold a collection of beaded cords which are not meant to be tied. A lucet-braided cord and beads decorate the edge of the Book.

The front cover (top photograph), and back cover and spine (bottom photograph).

ALCUIN OF YORK (d. 804) eighth-century scholar, native of Northumbria, refers to gifts of silk wall-hangings interwoven with gold that King Oswald of Northumbria presented to the churches he had founded, but this may refer to woven fabric from Byzantium rather than to English embroidery.

74

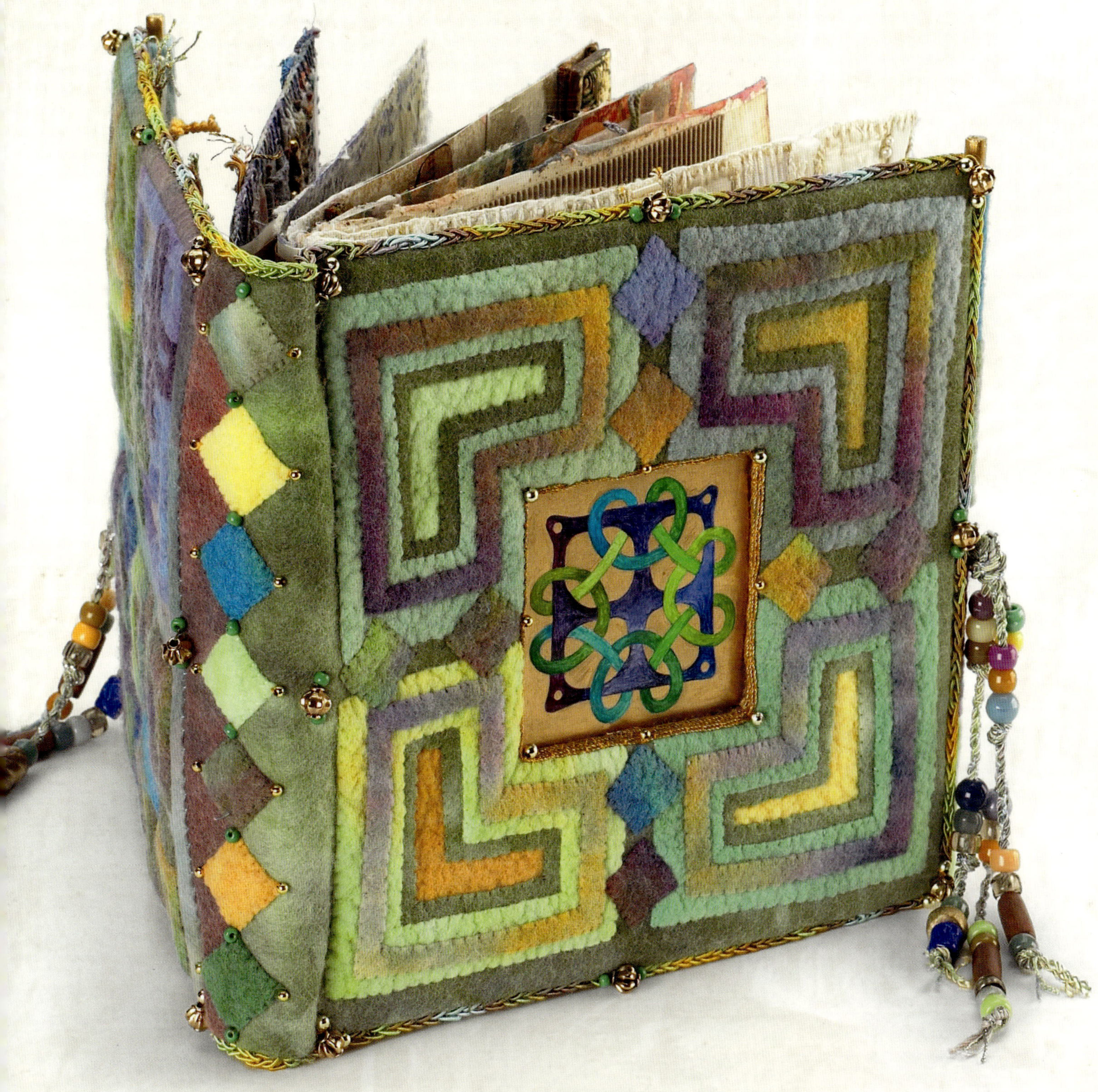
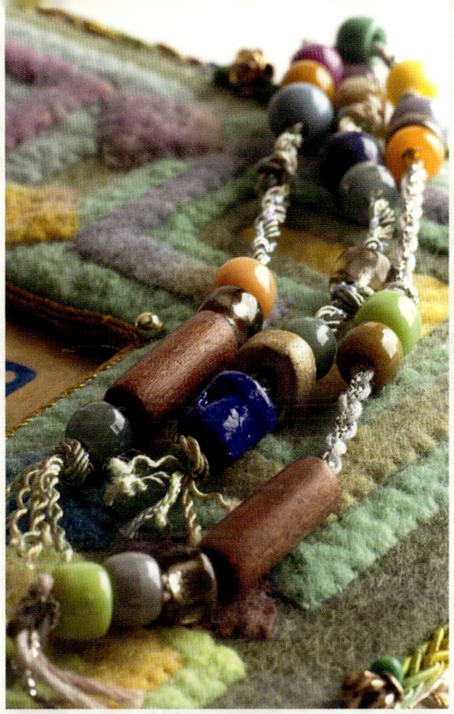
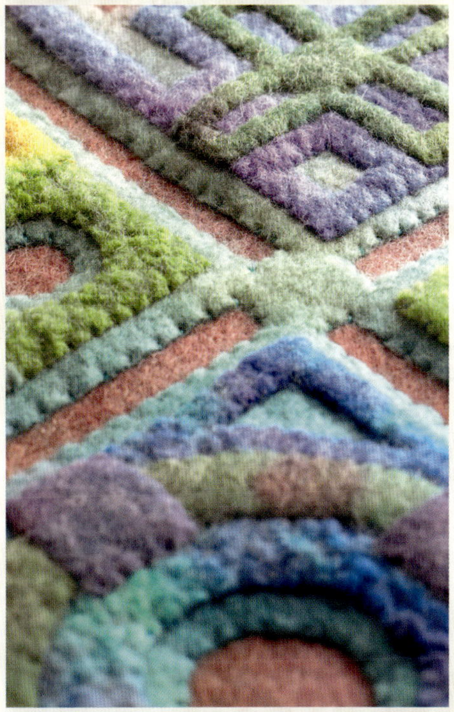
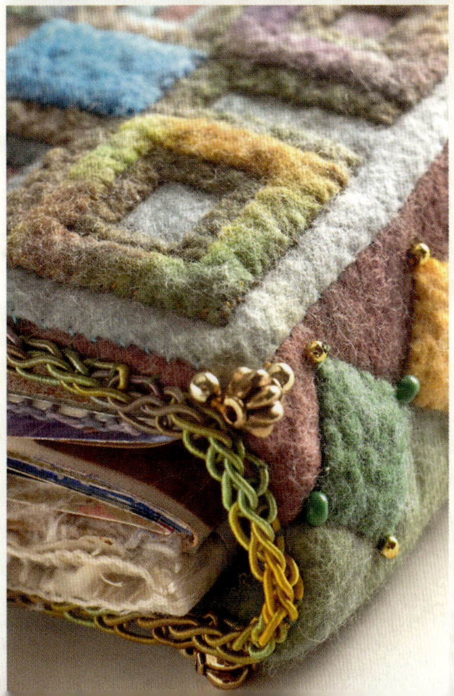

Inside front cover

This fabric fantasy represents a glimpse of the rich textures and remnants of decoration that might once have been seen on the garments of the nobility. Pearls, gold, beads and braids would have been much in evidence, and a collection of assorted strips, partly embroidered, suggests the antiquated opulence of rediscovered Anglo-Saxon garments.

Page one

Page two

Noblewomen of the tenth century would have possessed both the time and skills to decorate the borders of their gowns, and those of their menfolk, with embroidery. Taking a scheme of colours, one can play with this idea on a small scale through swatches of fabrics and papers, simple stitches and motifs, cords and jewels. The quatrefoil motif was well known, but many others can be adapted from the borders of the Bayeux Tapestry, from jewellery and manuscripts.

PAGE THREE

79

Page four

The background of runny paint is easily prepared by allowing brushfuls of wet colour to fall (vertically or horizontally) over a previously laid wet colour. To create more fusion of colour, spray water, paint or walnut ink on to the damp background.

The figure on the left wears a plain linen undergarment known as a smock, over which is worn a shorter tunic, or kirtle, with wider and shorter sleeves. The smock shows beneath this at the neck, arms and hem. The wool or linen tunic would have been worn girdled or loose, and it may also have been lined.

An extra garment, not shown here, is the super-tunic, or roc, from which is derived the modern word 'frock'. This was a loose garment sometimes hitched up into the girdle to show the kirtle beneath, often lined with silk or edged with fur.

For outdoors, there was also the mantle, either full-length and square-cut or perhaps semi-circular as shown on the right. Some would have been fastened with costly brooches of gold, silver and gems. Linings of a different colour were common in the later tenth century.

The fine linen or silk veil was essential wear for all women, consisting of a long wide scarf covering all the hair, neck and shoulders but worn in various ways with the ends hanging in front or behind. For the wealthy, jewelled headbands and gold circlets would also have been worn.

PAGE FIVE

Page six

An Anglo-Saxon man of the tenth century would have worn a collarless linen or woollen shirt under a straight tunic which may have been short, knee-length, or ankle-length for ceremonial occasions. The tunic varied in the degree of decoration, but it was usual for all edges, seams and necklines to be embroidered and for the belt or girdle to be richly ornamented. On occasion, noblemen would also have worn an outer tunic of silk or fine linen, and also a woollen cloak fastened by a brooch on the shoulder. Legs were either encased in breeches that tied at the waist, or in long 'braes' bound from knee to ankle with strips of fabric or leather thongs.

The tiny tunics on the left are made of hand-dyed felt and indicate where bands of embroidery would have been placed. The tiny scraps of postcard are from the Bayeux Tapestry Finale, an eight-foot-long panel which I made in 1996 to reconstruct the missing end of the real tapestry, now in Normandy. It shows the coronation of William the Conqueror in Westminster Abbey in 1066, and features men wearing best, ordinary and ecclesiastical costumes. The Bayeux Tapestry Finale is on view in the atrium of the James Cook Memorial Hospital, Middlesbrough, England.

Page seven

83

Page eight

English-made cloaks and mantles found their way to all corners of Christendom, often sent as costly gifts and marks of favour. The rather improbably patterned version worn by the figure of St Matthew from the Irish Book of Durrow suggests that it may represent a coloured plaid embellished by the artist's imagination. Having copied this immaculate little figure on a larger scale, I can testify to the astonishing skill of the seventh-century artist.

The hooded figure is probably from a Celtic or Pictish tribe. A trio of these figures was discovered at Housesteads on Hadrian's Wall, Northumberland, carved in high relief on a stone slab, well protected by their long woollen cloaks against the harsh northern winds. They may even have been lined with fleece.

The curly-haired figure of St Matthew is from another Irish gospel book, the Book of Kells. He wears a voluminous blanket-like mantle with decorated borders which may in fact have been tablet-woven braids.

Page nine

85

Page ten

We have no hard evidence that young Anglo-Saxon women, or Vikings, stitched practice-samplers as we did in later centuries; perhaps the materials were too costly for this. However, I imagine that Alditha or Aelfgyva would surely have tried out their stitches and techniques somewhere, so this is my version of what one may have looked like before young Alditha was allowed to adorn her father's tunic. It also gave me a chance to practise my own ideas!

PAGE ELEVEN
IMITATION TABLET
WEAVING

Tablet weaving was much used by the English and Scandinavians as an additional method of decorating textiles. Square 'tablets' of bone and ivory exactly like those used today have been found in graves alongside women's implements.

The long, narrow braids would have been woven from threads of wool, linen or silk, sometimes with gold, often with simple diamond or striped patterns or with more complex ones of animals and foliage that required a good memory on the part of the weaver. It was a slow process, so braids produced in this way were highly prized and often re-used on the garments of noblemen and women, royalty and on church vestments.

At a distance, imitation tablet weaving (closely worked rows of whipped running stitch) could pass for the real thing where the pattern is a simple stripe or border, but by using random-dyed (space-dyed) threads, the effect is even more convincing. On the hem to be decorated, begin by stitching several rows of running stitch one above the other with the space of one or two threads between each row. The stitches may be either stacked up in blocks or placed at random, though orderly blocks make the most convincing appearance when smooth threads are used (examples 1 and 4).

The running stitch thread can be either plain or multi-coloured, fine or coarse, depending on the scale of the braid required.

Next, using either the same or a thicker thread, 'whip' the running stitches using a blunt needle. The background fabric is entered only at the beginning and end of each row. For best effect, each row of whipping is made in the same direction (i.e. into the same part of the stitch) as shown in example 1, but fuzzy woollen threads tend to disguise such changes, as example 3 shows, so there is no hard-and-fast rule here.

Tips: don't pull the whipped thread too tightly, but let it wrap the running stitch like a wave. To keep running stitches in regular blocks, draw faint pencil lines. Use a thicker thread for the whipped part and allow it to spread sideways by using it double. Always use a blunt-ended tapestry needle for this. To make a fake-fur edging, whip the running stitches with a fuzzy knitting yarn in fur colours like white, grey, black or brown.

Thank you to Beryl Bickerstaffe for introducing me to this method of imitation tablet weaving and for allowing me to use it here.

ALDERET'S WIFE at Winchester. At her death in 1083, Queen Mathilde bequeathed to the Church of the Holy Trinity at Caen, 'the chasuble which is being embroidered at Winchester by Alderet's wife; the cloak wrought in gold, laid up in my chamber, to make a cope of … and another robe now being embroidered in England.' Alderet was an important thegn in Winchester, perhaps a moneyer from a family of goldsmiths.

The samples

1. Eight rows of stacked running stitches whipped with a thick random-dyed glossy silk thread used double. Double gold knitting yarn is used on the two centre rows. All the whipping is worked in the same direction.

2. Eleven rows of thick white/cream linen thread for the running stitch worked randomly. Top and bottom rows are double-whipped with a two-ply wool yarn, then a textured knitting yarn on top. Both used double. Beads added.

3. Twelve rows of closely worked running stitch, some in blocks, some random. Whipped with two-ply woollen yarn in all directions. Slub knitting yarn couched along top and bottom edges.

4. Striped fabric helps to position running stitch in blocks. Twelve rows of multi-coloured stranded cotton, whipped with white two-ply wool and gold knitting yarn, both doubled. Direction of whipped stitch was changed halfway and coloured beads sewn into spaces created by this.

5. Ten rows of close running stitch in random-dyed stranded cotton whipped with the same thread in alternate directions. Four of these rows were whipped again in the opposite direction with a single gold thread to accentuate the plaited effect. Beads are added along the lower edge.

89

PAGE TWELVE

Small labels illustrate the colourful richness of Anglo-Saxon clothing, the beading and gold ornament. Machine-stitching holds the fabrics together on Vilene shapes. The walnut-ink stained background shows excerpts from Domesday Book.

90

INSIDE BACK COVER

91

King Eadward's tunic

Supposing that a worksheet was needed for the king's approval, this is what it might have looked like: a selection of fabrics, a sample of the under-tunic cuff, the embroidery on neck, sleeves and hem, garnets hanging from the edge. Since King Eadward the Confessor is reputed to have been little interested in his appearance and more interested in hunting, it would no doubt have been his wife, Queen Edgyth, who made the decisions, especially as she was an expert embroiderer.

AELFGYTH (mentioned in Domesday Book, 1086) held land at Oakley in Buckinghamshire 'which Godric the sheriff granted to her to hold as long as he was sheriff, on condition of her teaching his daughter embroidery work'.

Green sleeve fragment

The kind of fragment one might find in a museum, belonging to a high-status lady of the tenth century. Appliqué, couching and quilting on hand-dyed silk.
Private collection.

AELFREDA'S GOWN FOR FEAST DAYS

Women's gowns were sure to have been ornamented on sleeves, neckline and hem, although whether they had loops and ties like this I do not know. Quilting they certainly knew, since the men wore heavy quilted-canvas gambesons beneath their chain mail. This fragment is of silks, cottons, papers and gold foil.
Private collection.

According to the chronicler, Thomas of Ely, ST ETHELDREDA (d. 679), also known as Aelthelthryth and Audrey, was abbess of the double monastery at Ely, Cambridgeshire founded in 673. She was the wife of Ecgfrith, King of Northumbria 670–85, her second husband. She offered to St Cuthbert of Lindisfarne a stole and maniple finely embroidered by herself and worked with gold and precious stones.

AETHELSTAN'S SUNDAY-BEST

King Aethelstan, King of the English from 925 to 939, was a great donor of books and land to various churches, a founder of monasteries, a law-giver and host to many foreign scholars. He presented the fine embroideries, made in Winchester, to the tomb of St Cuthbert, which can still be seen in Durham Cathedral.

He was buried in the Abbey at Malmesbury. This embroidered fragment represents part of Aethelstan's most sumptuous robe.
Private collection.

THE BOOK OF ANCIENT ACCESSORIES

INTRODUCTION

Graves have yielded up quantities of small items used to clasp sleeve openings, to buckle belts, to pin hair and cloaks, to finish off girdles and to hang from waists. Bits of shoes have been found, combs and tweezers, purse fastenings and things that might have been this or that, vaguely labelled 'artefacts'. Historians often disagree.

The best places to see these things are, of course, museums, where one can appreciate the scale and sheer artistry that went into the production of accessories, telling us quite clearly that our ancient ancestors were just as careful of their appearance as we are today. It is not true, apparently, that Viking men were unkempt and unwashed. On the contrary, they were proud of their bathing facilities and of their long hair which they plaited in a variety of styles, even their beards. Combs made from antler have been found in great quantities, used by men as much as by women. Englishmen were derided by Normans for their long flowing locks and moustaches, but they were wearing them too, before long, as well as the jewellery and shoes with pointed toes. In nunneries, women were scolded by letters from their bishops for having long nails like talons, for wearing red shoes and jewelled veils, for spending too long on their embroidery instead of their prayers, and for wearing jewellery and rouge.

The theme of ancient accessories may be an attractive one to those who enjoy making small items like embroidered postcards, greetings cards, little books, boxes, purses, pincushions and cases for scissors or spectacles. Ancient designs fit these shapes very well. For extra authenticity, though, the choice of colour can help, as these were obtained from natural sources, not the harsh palette of today's chemical colours. It is true that they liked bright colours, but try soft madder reds, sap greens, ochres and russets, elderberry greys and soft mauves, lichen colours, onion-skin yellows and woad or indigo blues (faded denim colours).

Tassels are an essential part of this chapter, as they can be simple and small or massively elaborate. Although most ancient examples have perished over the centuries, a few stunning discoveries have been preserved in peat bogs, demonstrating how much time and effort was expended on this ubiquitous accessory. Beads, plaits and pendants can also add glamour to even the simplest piece of embroidery, particularly when made to the appropriate scale.

OUTSIDE

Designed to display bulky tassels, this folder has two 'pages', two wide spines, and an overlapping piece to fold over and close. The cover is very simple: strips of assorted cottons and silks were attached to iron-on Vilene, then sewn down by machine using both straight and zig-zag stitches. The assembled piece was then cut into three sections across the strips, re-arranged, then re-assembled by machine. The strapwork design was embroidered by hand in gold thread using satin stitch over a template of medium-weight Vilene stuck to the background. Extra hand-embroidery and beads were added for colour and richness.

Sometimes it is difficult to transfer a pattern on to a background, especially if the pattern is intricate and the background bumpy. So I use a template of Vilene. First, I trace the pattern on to a piece of plastic craft parchment or vellum, using a fine fibre-pen. Then, with a fine craft knife, I cut the pattern out on a cutting mat. The resulting template can be re-used many times. I then lay the template on to white medium-weight Vilene and draw round it, then I cut the Vilene shape out with the craft knife to obtain a second template which is to be stitched over.

Before sticking the Vilene to the background fabric, it must be painted, usually the same colour as the thread you wish to use. Take care to paint the cut edges too, as these will otherwise show white. If you are using a strapwork pattern, mark the overlaps before you stitch.

Use a fabric glue to stick the template to your background, then hold it permanently in place with satin stitches (regular or irregular) that only pierce the background, not the template.

The ties of the folder are more decorative than functional. Simple two-element twisted cords are hitched on to the D-ring, the ends enclosed inside a narrow felt tube hung with beads. Originally these were large glass beads with wide holes, big enough to take threads wrapped round the outside. A small petal-shaped jewellery 'finding' with a loop at the top was stuck to each bead, hung with a tiny metal ring and sewn to the end of each tube. Self-adhesive gold foil tape, ¼in (0.5cm) wide, was wrapped round each end to finish it off. This tape is very useful for enclosing the loose ends of cords.

INSIDE

Tassels and fringes were well used by even the earliest embroiderers, the fringe being the left-over warp threads along the top and bottom edges of handwoven fabric, tied into bunches to prevent unravelling. The red tassel on the left-hand side of the folder is based on a Bronze-Age (c. 1700 B.C.) girdle tassel made of horse-hair, where the thick bunch of fibres is divided, wrapped and sub-divided before being weighted with coloured glass beads. The gold bands and top-knot are my own addition, but the original, found in Ireland, was probably just as splendid.

The heavier tassel in the centre of the folder is bound at the top with large wrapped rings made on a cardboard tube, and smaller rings made on a cordonne stick. Using strips of gilded leather, more tassels are tied in, the top covered with buttonhole stitch and crowned with a flat, bound ring.

The fringe in the background was knotted on to painted strips of corrugated cardboard placed against a pin-tucked fabric meant to echo the vertical theme. Hanging labels are cut from a postcard, the edges painted gold, and hung on twisted cords. The elongated bead is simply rolled felt wrapped in gold lace and sewn with tear-drop beads.

Cords (shown on the right-hand side of the folder) were universally used for fastenings, as were brooches, pins, hooks and buckles. Today's fastenings, buttons, zips and press-studs were not known, and although there is no reason why one cannot incorporate these into historic themes, I prefer to use what was there at that time. Probably the cheapest and commonest fastenings were ties made of leather strips, twisted and plaited cords made from animal and plant fibres, and woven cords made on primitive looms. Only the simplest are included here. From right to left, they are: finger braids, made on the fingers with either one or two elements; a plait using four elements; a plait using three elements of the same or similar thickness; fine twisted cords with tubes of wrapped felt attached to the ends; lucet cords, which are made on an ancient tool, known as a lucet, that produces a square rather than a flat braid (see page 105); twisted cords using one and two different elements.

Other ideas for cords include those made with a machined zig-zag stitch over threads; coloured strings bound with gold wire; knotted strips of fabric or bundles of threads; and cord enclosed within a tube of fabric, rolled and hand-sewn. These can all be further decorated with beads, charms, feathers, tassels and pom-poms.

99

ANCIENT BEADS

(Not drawn to scale.)

Of all the artefacts found in the graves of Anglo-Saxon and Viking women, the most plentiful are beads, highly prized for their beauty as well as their worth as charms and amulets. The pendant 'gripping beast' motif made of jet, and the silver cross above it, would have been worn round the neck, though it was also usual to suspend a string of beads between two brooches where they could all be seen on a woman's chest.

In the eighth century, many Viking towns and trading centres, Ribe in Denmark, for instance, had glass-bead-making craftsmen. In Britain, however, only York is known to have had glass workshops at this time, although beads are known to have been produced in Co. Cork, Ireland. The coloured glass would, for the most part, have been imported from Northern Italy as a raw material, as unused mosaic pieces, waste and broken drinking vessels. This would have been re-heated, moulded, twisted or fused into various shapes by skilled craftsmen.

The large polychrome bead at the top left of the page was probably made in Ireland during the seventh to ninth centuries, though it was found during excavations in York. The six polychrome beads below this were discovered in Lincolnshire, while the large cylindrical emerald from York belongs to the mid-eighth to ninth centuries and is thought to be of Roman origin, probably mined in Egypt.

Other materials were made into beads too. Stone, bone, shell, jet, amber, rock crystal, metals, garnet and cornelian. Seen at the top centre, amber was much favoured as pendants, beads and amulets because it could be carved into specific shapes according to the need. Deposits of amber were found on the shores of the Baltic Sea from where it was exported to the rest of Europe, some also being found in western Denmark.

York soon became an important production centre of amber goods. Some amber was actually washed on to the east coast of Britain, but Whitby, a town on Yorkshire's eastern coastline, had its own exclusive and valuable material known at the time as 'black amber', now known as jet: dense, black and easily carved. Rock crystal and cornelian were both imported from areas around the Black Sea, amethyst from the Continent and the Far East.

The necklace on the left in the painting is of rock crystal and cornelian hung with trinkets of silver, gold and glass. It was found at Birka in Sweden where it may once have belonged to a Viking woman of some wealth. The two elaborate polychrome glass beads in the centre of the page are from Ribe in Denmark, while some of the smaller beads belong to the Pagan Lady of Peel collection. Found in a grave on St Patrick's Isle on the Isle of Man, they are thought to have belonged to a Viking woman of the pre-Christian era.

The necklace of handmade and bought beads, made by the author, represents an ancient Anglo-Saxon version, though the large chunks of amber come from Ethiopia rather than Europe. Those beads painted to imitate lapis lazuli were made from modelling clay; others were bought from craft shops.

101

Anglo-Saxon fragments box

This box of bits and pieces, measuring 10in (25cm) square, represents my response to those small, unidentifiable fragments displayed in museums, often still tangled or embedded in other materials. A tangle of gold wires or a ring, tiny scraps of fabric and stitching, bits of glass and metal foil, ends of belts and hanging things, an old brooch mount and a twisted pin, none of them very lovely in isolation yet precious and significant because of their relationship to those who made and used them.

Basic compartment boxes are available in large craft stores, usually meant for displaying collections. When spray-painted inside and out, one of these can house small pieces of embroidery related by theme, colour or technique.

Each of the large squares measures 5 x 5in (12.5 x 12.5cm). The embroidery on the background fabric is mounted over card and glued in place. The small squares of embroidery are better displayed by being set flush with the wooden dividers, so to prevent them falling inwards, I glued a small square of foam behind each one, then glued this to the base. The glass cover is hinged at the top.

103

Purses and pouches

All women from whatever era needed some kind of pouch, purse or satchel to carry personal items: combs, spindle-whorls, keys, tweezers, coins, amulets and shears. This would have hung from a belt or girdle, but before the seventh century it was common for British women to wear their tools on a chain known as a chatelaine. Viking women often wore girdle-hangers as a mark of their social importance, though it is not understood whether these were functional or merely ornamental.

Shapes of small purses have mostly been gathered from the artwork of the time, as intact examples have rarely survived, only the metal fittings. Artwork, however, does not show us exactly how these bags were constructed, so most of those seen here are reconstructions based on fragments, clasps and strap-ends. We are more sure of the pouch seen on the left of the picture, an Anglo-Saxon style made from a rectangle of fabric, sometimes leather, and perhaps lined, gathered and attached to a ring of bone, ivory or metal. The pouch with the metal clasps shown top right is also of the Anglo-Saxon period, as is the satchel at bottom left, made of leather and decorated with a metal medallion.

MAHALT (c. 1050), also known as Maud/ Mathilde: 'Mahalt she was called and she was a worker; marvellously did she know how to work, to embroider fine gold upon purple silk, to ornament with regal jewels. She knew how to place gems and good stones better than anyone before her. Her fame in this was such that she was sought after by the highest nobles, honoured and demanded for her art.'

La vie d'Edourard le confesseur

The lucet

This device, about 5in (12.5cm) long and made of wood, bone, walrus ivory or antler, is for making a four-sided cord. The small extra piece (shown on the right of the picture) fits over the forks to keep the loops in place when not in use. Although we have no hard evidence that the lucet was used by Anglo-Saxon or Viking women in Britain, an implement that may have been one of these devices in-the-making was discovered in York in the area occupied by Vikings. Many textile historians believe that the lucet is a very ancient tool.

To make a cord, choose a strong, smooth thread for a start. Fine string is ideal. Nothing too slippery.

1. Thread the lucet as shown in the first diagram, then take hold of it in your left hand, placing your little finger on the neck at the base. Place your thumb on the left-hand loop and trap the working thread (i.e. the loose thread attached to your ball of yarn) between your first two fingers. This keeps the thread under tension.

2. Use the fingers of your right hand to lift the lower of the two threads on the right-hand fork up and over the working thread. Let it drop down to the other side, as you do in knitting. Now turn the lucet round in your left hand (see the arrows) while gently pulling the working thread across to the right, laying it across the right-hand fork as shown. This will tighten the knot and prepare for the next one.

3. With the lucet now facing the other way in your left hand, lift the lower right-hand-side yarn up and over the working yarn again (i.e. over the fork), turn the lucet and pull the thread across once more. The lucet is turned in the left hand each time a new knot is made, ready to make the next one. All the action takes place on the right-hand side. As the knots begin to pile up in the centre, pull the cord down gently through the holes.

Note: you may find it easier to lift the lower thread with a stiletto, a bodkin, or a fine crochet hook.

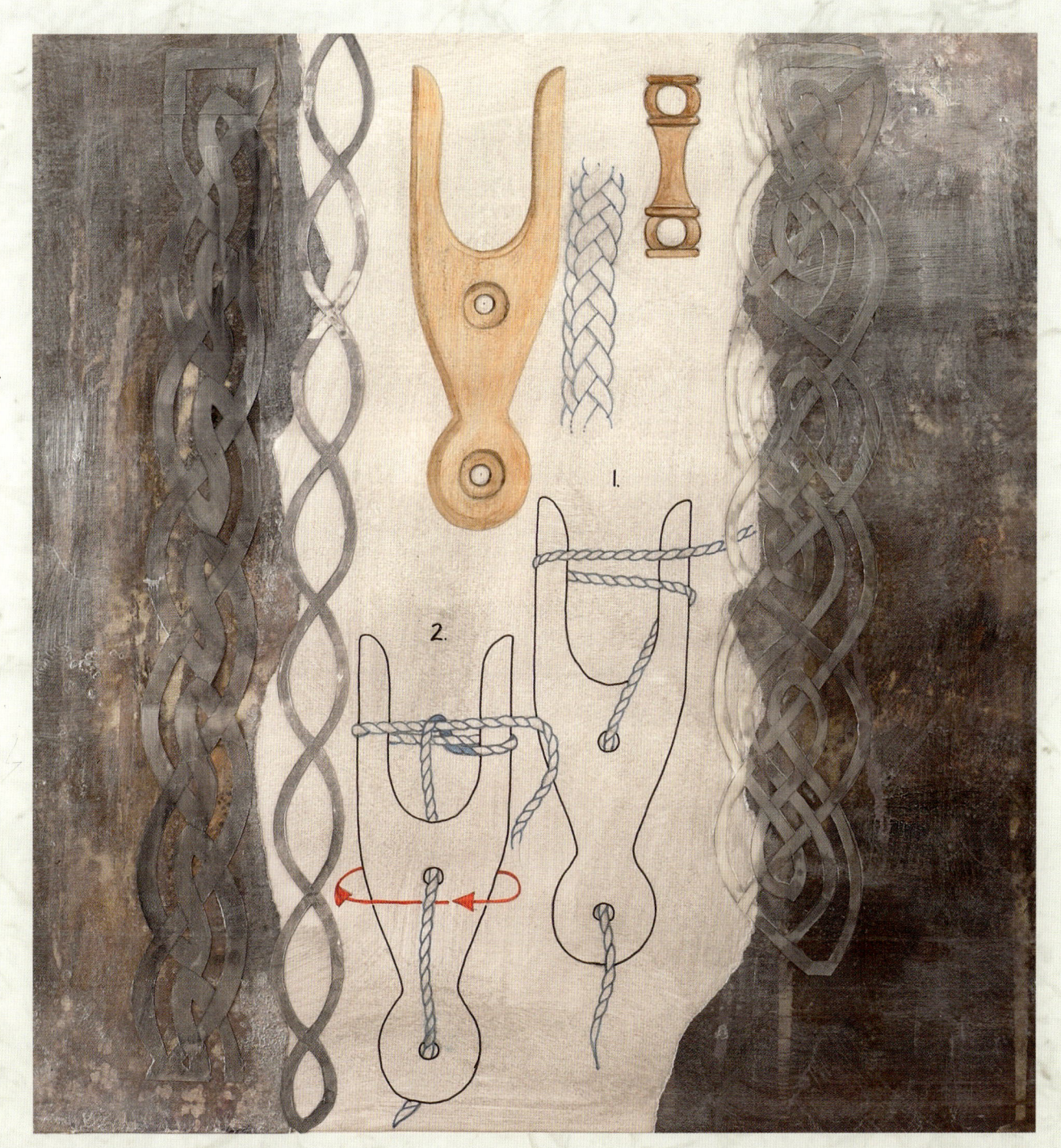

Four Anglo-Saxon purses

Purple purse
10½ x 6in (27 x 15cm)

Fabric: silk cover and lining.

Embroidery: a band of brocaded gold overlaid with chevrons and triangles of Bayeux stitch; couched and beaded gold cords.

Top: bound with gold fabric, elasticated; beads and tassels.

Ivory/silver purse
10 x 5in (25.5 x 12.5cm)

Fabric: ivory silk with bands of darker silk and silver bias binding.

Embroidery: Celtic motif in stem stitch and variegated silks; herringbone and couching; typical Anglo-Saxon border design at base.

Lining: mauve silk.

Top: bound with hand-dyed silk couched with silver cord. Mauve cord couched all round top, tied at the front over a silver medallion. Bought silver tassels topped with silver 'tops', further decorated with beads.

Orange purse
9 x 4 in (23 x 10cm)

Fabric: silk and metallic scraps fused to a silk background, embellished by machine.

Embroidery: couched with extra metallic threads and tied scraps.

Lining: cotton printed with Celtic knotwork pattern.

Top: bound with leather shoelace; metal D-rings bound with gold thread looped on to narrow strips, ends tucked between lining and cover.

White purse
8½ x 5in (21.5 x 12.5cm)

Fabric: slub silk.

Embroidery: machine-applied bands of figured gauze, ribbons, gold bias binding, gold cords and beads; diamond shapes of chain stitch in variegated silks show between vertical stripes.

Lining: grey silk.

Top: white, fake-ivory Indian bracelet bound to a gathered edge; tassels buttonholed with gold thread and beads.

INSTRUCTIONS FOR MAKING UP

Materials needed: pieces of sturdy fabric for the outer cover and suitable lining fabric to the same dimensions as the pattern; embroidery threads etc.

1. Trace the two patterns and cut them out. Lay the pattern for the outer cover on to your fabric and pin it in place. Tack all round the shape and remove the template. Work any embroidery at this stage before cutting the fabric. Use a frame if necessary. When the embroidery is complete, cutting out can begin, but remember that no seam allowances have been included on the pattern, so you will need to add ½in (1cm) all round.

2. Without the embroidery, do the same with the lining pattern and fabric. It is usual to make the lining a fraction smaller than the outer cover, and also to stiffen the shape with interfacing. However, I did neither of these things with my four purses, so the choice is yours.

3. With right sides together, seam the outer cover up the back, press the seam open, then fold it, as indicated, with right sides together, so that the scoop is at the front. Sew it across the lower edge and turn it to the right side.

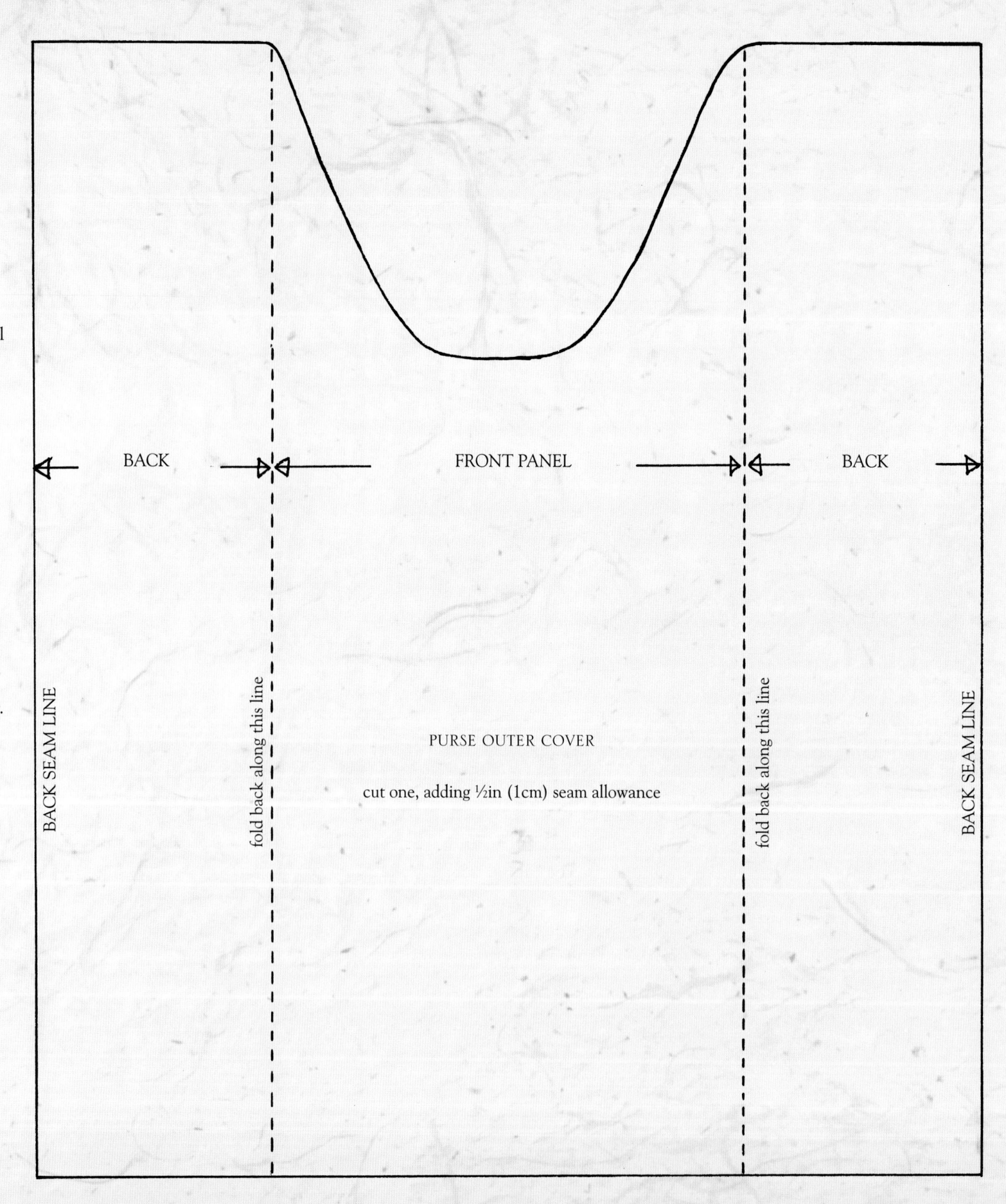

BACK SEAM LINE | fold back along this line | BACK | FRONT PANEL | BACK | fold back along this line | BACK SEAM LINE

PURSE OUTER COVER

cut one, adding ½in (1cm) seam allowance

4. Do the same with the lining, but remember that the seam will be at the front, hidden from view. This piece stays inside out. Slip it inside the outer cover, adjusting the corners and curves to fit.

5. On the outer cover, turn down the seam allowance, snipping the inner curves. Pin, then tack. Do the same with the lining, snipping the front inner curves and folding the allowance towards the outer cover so that the lining sits just below it. Tack this piece also. Note: if you prefer to bind the top edges, there will be no need to fold them in. Use a bias-cut strip of fabric and join it at the back.

6. Pin the two sections together and hand-sew them with an invisible stitch. A cord may be couched down over this edge or, before completing the back section, tabs may be added like those shown in the examples. The ends of these are tucked between the back cover and the lining. Alternatively, a cord long enough to pass over a person's head and to hang down the front will make the purse into a spectacles case.

7. Add any suitable embellishment, card, beads, tassels, etc.

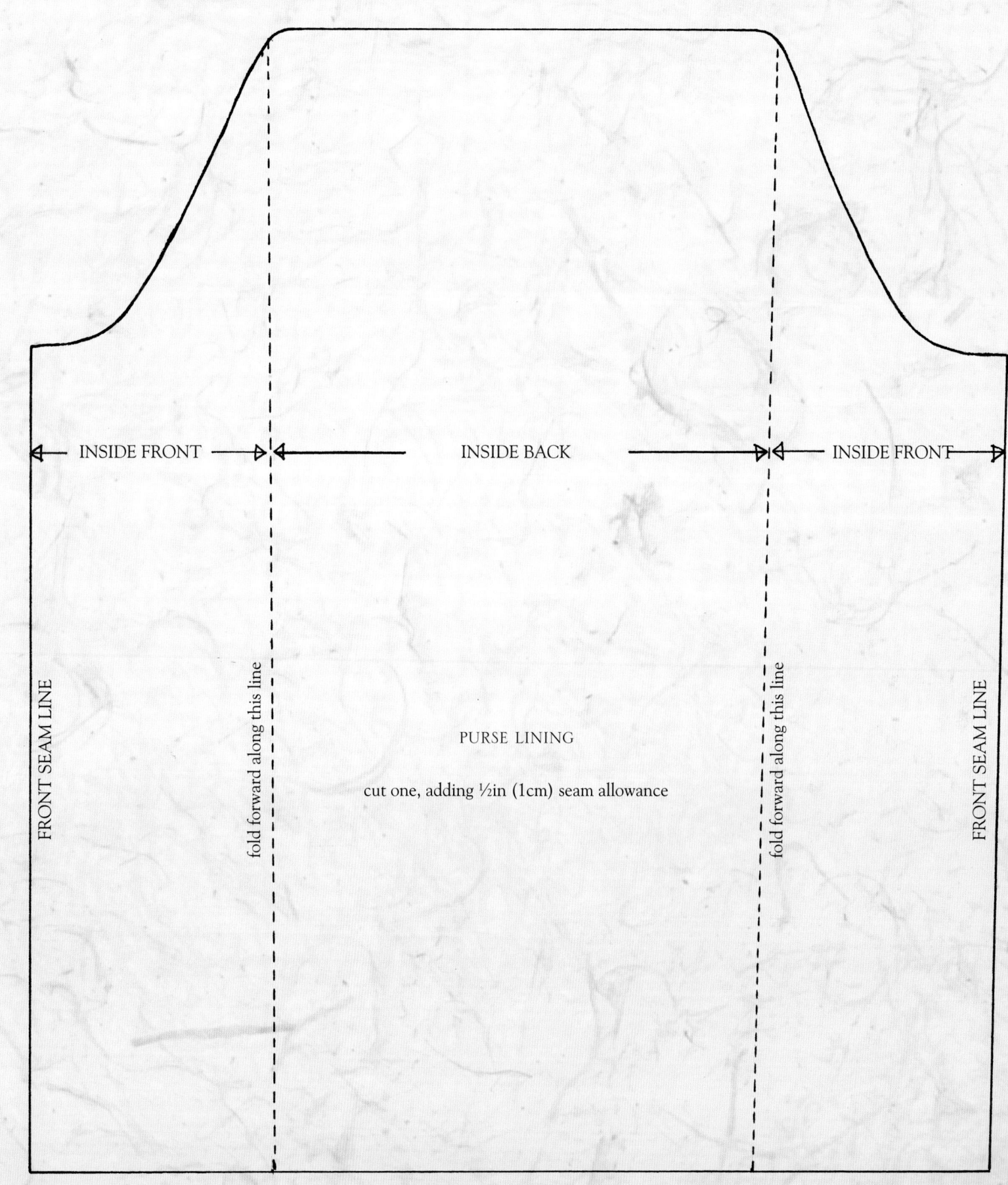

← INSIDE FRONT → ← INSIDE BACK → ← INSIDE FRONT →

FRONT SEAM LINE

fold forward along this line

PURSE LINING

cut one, adding ½in (1cm) seam allowance

fold forward along this line

FRONT SEAM LINE

109

The workbox book

The basic box is made of strong papier-mâché and can be purchased from any large craft store in a variety of sizes. This one measures 8 x 5½ x 2in (20 x 14 x 5cm) and was originally the colour of brown paper before I painted it with acrylics in various golds, blues, greens and browns. The three sides meant to represent the pages were painted a muddy white, the colour of old parchment.

To decorate the covers further, I cut a design out of thin gold card to the pattern of an Anglo-Saxon gospel book which had semi-precious stones set into it. At this time, stones were always cabochon-cut, not facetted, but I had to make do with flat-sided fake jewels and beads. The gold settings surrounding the jewels are stick-on transfers that can be bought in sheets from craft shops. The clasp is made from folded gold card, painted and punched, with cords, beads, card tabs and beaded tassels.

The inside must also be decorated, painted where it will not be covered by the lining. A gold-leaf marker pen is useful for touching up narrow edges. The four inner walls are lined with mottled green paper, as the intended fabric lining prevented the lid from closing. The base is lined with hand-quilted silk laced over card cut to the same dimensions. The lid was already fitted with a three-sided lip, perfect for a pincushion. The card base of the pincushion was cut to the same measurements, covered with hand-dyed felt over a layer of thick wadding, then laced into position. This was then glued to the lid.

The woven notebook

The cover of this notebook, measuring 5 x 4in (12.5 x 10cm) is an oblong of needleweaving worked on single canvas. This can be quite easily worked in the hand, although a temporary binding of masking tape will help to prevent woollen yarns snagging on the edges. My stitches were worked to within two threads of the canvas edge.

Materials needed: a piece of single canvas with about 12 to 14 holes per inch, measuring 5 x 9½in (12.5 x 24cm); a notebook (bought or made) to fit this size; a piece of felt to the same dimensions, plus two extra pieces for the pockets measuring 5 x 1¾in (12.5 x 4.5cm); strips of felt for the binding; woollen threads; crewel or three-ply knitting yarns; a blunt-ended tapestry needle; matching sewing cotton, gold cord, beads or other embellishments; masking tape to bind the edges of the canvas during working.

1. Using the holes and the stiffness of the canvas like a loom, lay rows of threads in small blocks, either horizontal or vertical. These should lie straight, but should not be pulled so tightly as to distort the canvas, each block butting up closely to the adjacent ones.

2. With either the same thread or a different one, weave across the laid threads, taking the needle into the canvas only at the beginning and end of each row. Each new row starts from the hole next to the previous row. Nudge the weft rows up to keep the lines straight. If you find that they will not pack together neatly, use a finer thread.

3. When all the canvas is covered, remove the masking tape from the edges. It is now ready to be lined with the felt. Take the two smaller pieces of felt and pin them to the front and back edges of the lining to form pockets into which the notebook endpapers can be slipped to hold the book in place. (Note: when the notebook is full, another one can be made to take its place.) Now take the lining-plus-pockets and lay it on the reverse side of the canvaswork cover. Pin, then tack all round, adjusting the edges.

4. Treating the cover and lining as one piece of fabric, bind the edges with the four strips of felt cut to the same length as each side, and no less than 1in (2.5cm) wide. Attach the two long sides first, then the short sides, overlapping the corners without mitring. This can be done by either hand or machine, or a combination of the two with the hand-stitching on the inside. Any kind of decoration can be added at this stage, for example a gold (doubled) cord, beads, a clasp, cords and tassels.

Scissors case and needlecase

I would like to think that early embroiderers made small pouches of leather in which to keep their needlework shears, though how they kept their precious needles safe is by no means certain, in spite of the small metal containers found (rarely) amongst grave-goods. Even so, I believe they would recognise both of these cases, as well as the Celtic spiral pattern that decorates them.

No pattern is needed for the spiral: just take double gold cord, start at the centre, and spiral round and round with the space of a cord thickness between rows. Keep the couching stitches fairly close together as this helps to make a better shape. I used two strands of fine variegated silk to couch the gold, but stranded cotton works just as well. Hand-dyed felt was used for both cases as this needs no turning of edges. The lining is silk, sewn over Vilene before being attached to the felt cover. Instructions can be found on the following pages.

LADY AELTHELSWITHA (c. 1050), daughter of King Cnut and Queen Emma (or perhaps his first wife), 'rejected marriage, and was assigned Coveney, Cambridgeshire, a place near the monastery (of Ely) where in retirement she devoted herself, with her maids, to gold embroidery. At her own cost and with her own hands, being extremely skilled in the craft, she made a white chasuble.'

A beautifully embroidered white headband is also mentioned in an inventory of the cathedral's goods, made by the Lady Aelthelswitha.

112

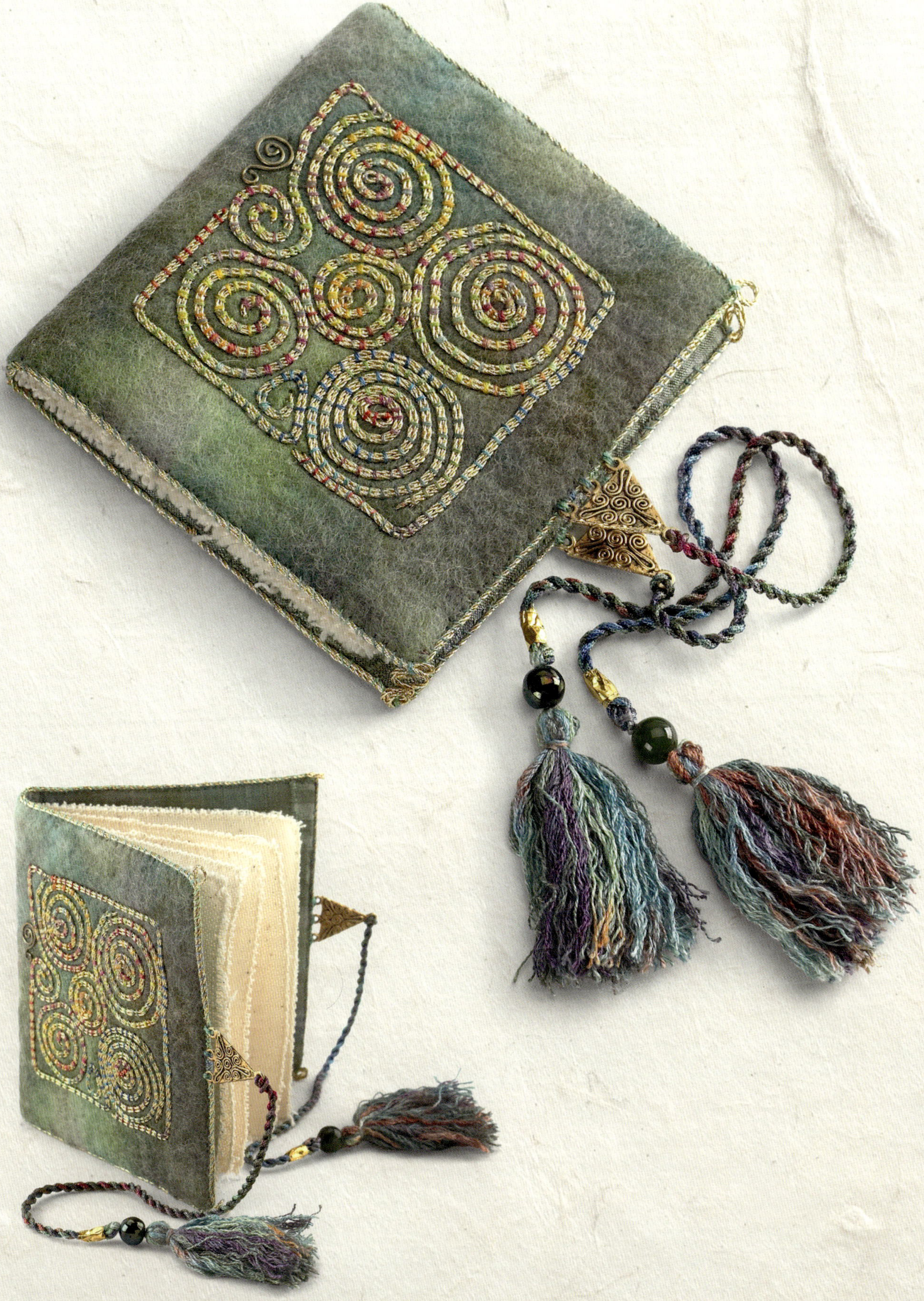

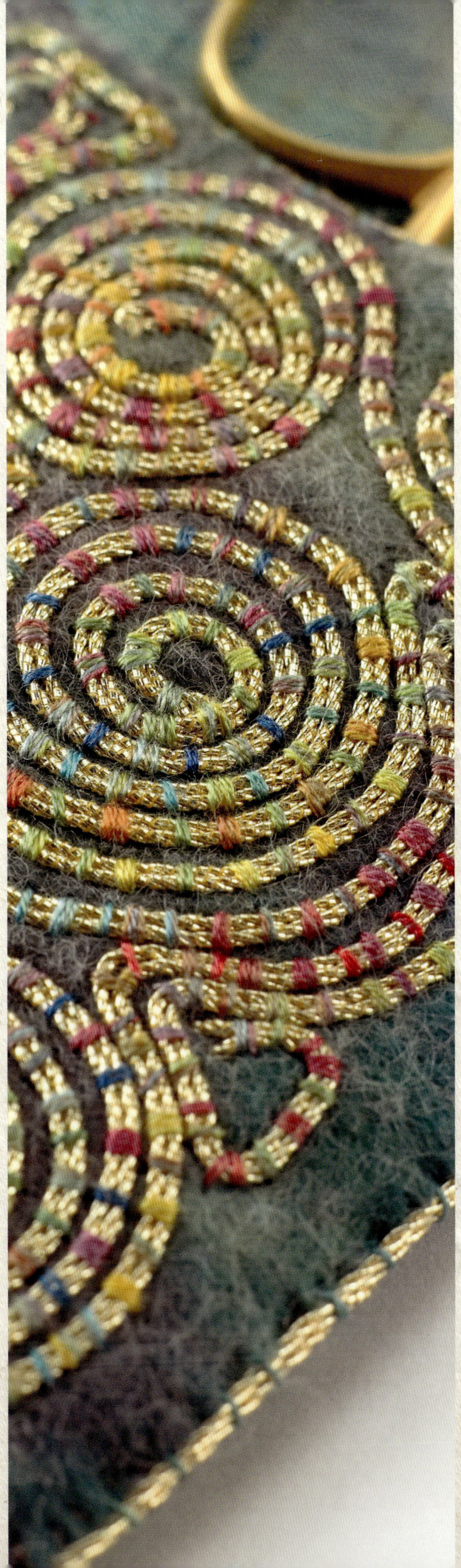

Instructions for making up

Materials needed: pieces of coloured felt, the size of the diagram; medium-weight Vilene; lining fabric; gold couching threads, embroidery silks or cotton, sewing cotton, needles and beads, matching threads to make cords; white felt or wool flannel for the needlecase pages.

Scissors case

1. Using the two shapes, cut out a pattern in both paper and Vilene. Pin the paper pattern to the felt and mark round the edge of each shape with small tacking stitches. It is helpful to use an embroidery frame at this stage. Remove the paper pattern.

2. Work embroidery on the front section and, if you wish, work a smaller motif on the back too, high up on the widest part.

SCISSORS CASE

BACK

cut one fabric and one lining, adding ½in (1cm) seam allowance

SCISSORS CASE

FRONT

cut one fabric and one lining, adding ½in (1cm) seam allowance

3. Pin the Vilene shapes to the lining fabric and, leaving a seam allowance of ½in (1cm) all round, cut the shapes out. Removing the pins as you reach them, turn the allowance over the edge of the Vilene, pin it again and tack it in place, mitring the points at the base.

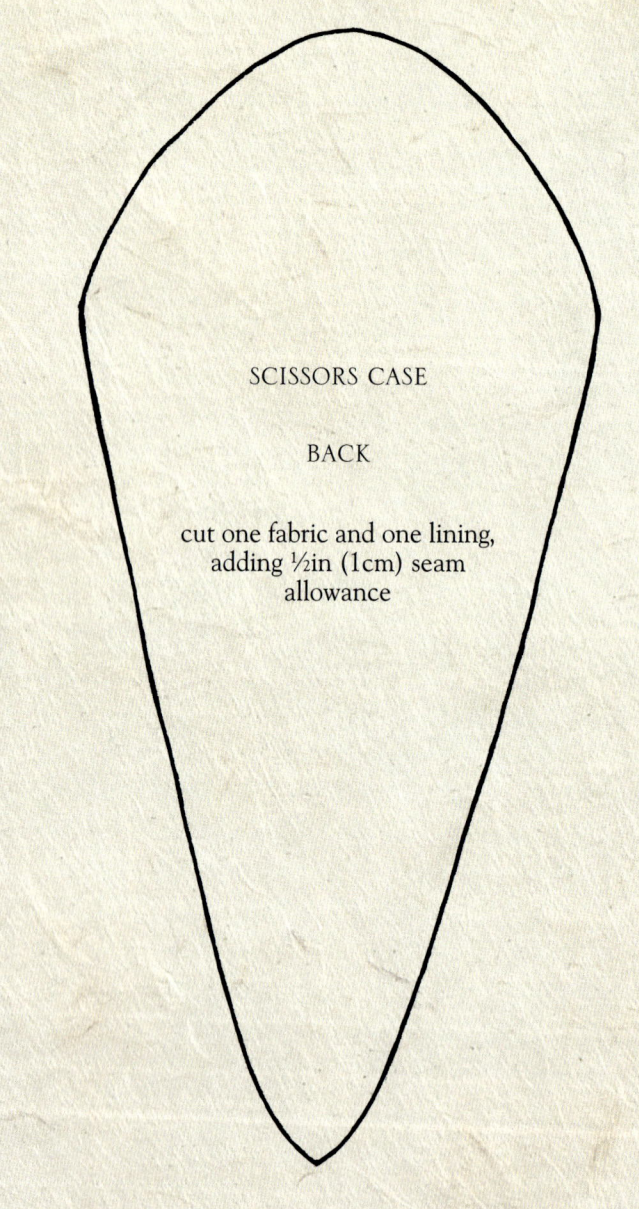

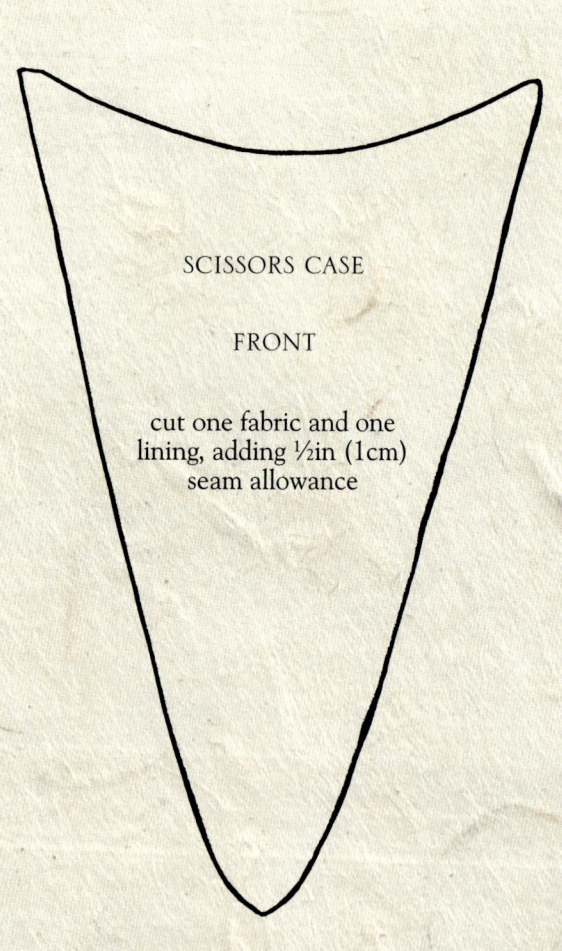

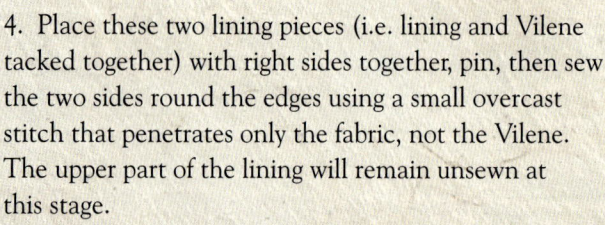

4. Place these two lining pieces (i.e. lining and Vilene tacked together) with right sides together, pin, then sew the two sides round the edges using a small overcast stitch that penetrates only the fabric, not the Vilene. The upper part of the lining will remain unsewn at this stage.

5. On the felt outer cover, leave an allowance of ½in (1cm) beyond the tacked outline, cut out the two shapes and lay them together, right sides out. Pin them, then stitch the two edges together using a small overcast stitch into the edges. To make this join even more secure, I turn back when I reach the end and sew round again in the opposite direction, making the stitches cross each other. The extra allowance is needed to accommodate the lining.

6. Place the lining into the felt 'pocket' and adjust it so that all edges meet. The back upper section will now be a little larger than the lining, so this should be trimmed off close to the lining edge. Pin it first.

7. Using a small overcast stitch, sew the front edge of the felt to the lining, then proceed round the top edge, sewing the felt cover and the lining together. Remove the tacking stitches.

8. Embellish the scissors case in any way you wish. I couched double gold braid all round the one shown here, working the front edge first. Then the twisted neck-cord was added. Beads and metal bits hang from the point, though tassels are an alternative.

Needlecase
Finished size 4 x 4in (10 x 10cm)

1. Make a paper oblong 4 x 8in (10 x 20cm), or thereabouts. Cut a Vilene shape to the same dimensions, then cut a lining which has an extra allowance of ½in (1cm) all round. Using the paper shape, pin it to the felt and mark it with tacking stitches, but do not cut it out yet.

2. Work your embroidery in a square on one side of the felt oblong, bearing in mind that, if your design has a right way up, it should be worked on the right-hand side of the oblong.

3. Pin the Vilene shape on to the lining fabric, then fold the lining allowance over the edges, mitre the corners and tack in place. Be precise.

4. Apply this piece to the inner side of the embroidered felt cover and pin them together. If the felt needs trimming, do this sparingly. Now stitch the two pieces together through the edges but not through the Vilene, using a very small overcast stitch in matching cotton.

5. Fold the oblong in half to make the book cover, then cut out fabric 'pages' of white felt or flannel to fit just inside the edges. Like the cover, these are simply three oblongs folded down the middle. By either hand or machine, stitch the pages together down the centre fold before fixing them to the cover. This helps to keep them in position. Then, using a thread that matches the cover, stitch all the way through pages and cover.

6. To finish off, couch a gold cord all the way round, beginning and ending on the bottom edge. Fastenings may be like the one shown, with twisted cords, or a buttonhole loop and bead.

Shoes and two figures

As far as we know, shoes and boots of the Anglo-Saxon and Viking periods were made of leather, varying in quality, cut and decoration. There was no difference in shoes for right and left feet, nor did the earliest ones have soles and uppers attached in the way our modern shoes do. Some of them resembled moccasins in this respect. Later on, they became more elaborate in style, although in the artwork of the time (our chief source of information), women's footwear tends to be hidden from view and the men's lacks sufficient detail.

During excavations in York, Viking footwear has been discovered resembling the boots shown here, while others appear to have had projecting 'tongues' like those worn in my painting of King Harold (shown below right). The shoemaker, or *sceowyrhta* in Old English, wears very stout shoes, his legs covered with woollen or linen strips wound round the legs and bound with thongs. The king also wore this kind of leg-covering, but here he wears striped socks, though it is not certain how these were kept up. See the Bayeux Tapestry for examples of men's leg-coverings. A sock made by the method known as nalebinding can be seen in the Viking Museum at York, most likely made by a Viking woman. Perhaps she had a sock shop there.

The diaper patterns behind the shoes are typical of the Anglo-Saxon and early medieval periods, based entirely on squares. Think of these as couched, stem-stitched or chain-stitched lines over appliqué to decorate purses or needlecases.

QUEEN AELFFLAED (d. 916), daughter of Queen Ealhswith (who founded the Nunnaminster at Winchester) and of King Alfred. It was here where a set of vestments was made 'at the command of Aelfflaed' for Bishop Frithestan of Winchester (909–931). In 934, the stole, maniple and girdle were presented by King Aethelstan (Aelfflaed's step-son) to the shrine of St Cuthbert when it rested at Chester-le-Street in Northumberland. These were found in the saint's coffin, and are now known as the Durham Vestments.

King Harold's cloak for Hastings

Continuing my theme of reconstructed fragments for certain Anglo-Saxons, this opulent piece measures 17 x 15in (43 x 38cm) and represents the cloak worn by King Harold, our last Anglo-Saxon king, when he rode to Hastings to meet William the Bastard. My attempt to recreate the patterns and textures have included techniques not known at the time; knitting and crochet, for example. Darning on single canvas is a useful way of imitating colourful patches of weaving, as shown here. The edges of the canvas can be either left exposed, painted, or covered by fabric.

Other patches include hand-dyed felt, coloured muslin and scraps of silk but, apart from the darning and freestyle knitting and crochet, there is hardly any stitching at all.

Author's collection

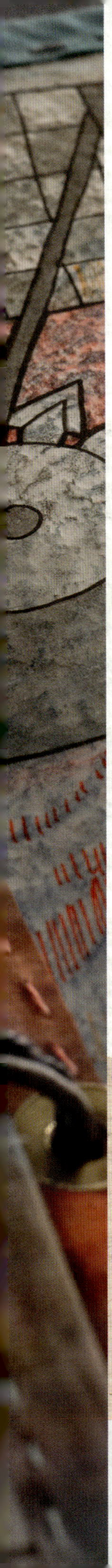

The Book of Motifs

Introduction

The covers of this Book, measuring 9 x 9½in (23 x 24cm), are of strong card to which are glued pieces of textured (bought) card painted with thick acrylic paint in blues, greys and metallic copper. The back cover shows how this looks without the extra decoration on the front, a net made entirely of freestyle crochet using metallic threads. This has been stretched across the shape and secured in places by a few stitches into the binding on the other side. The ties are made from twisted knitting wool and a heavy braid decorated with copper-painted beads and wooden toggles bought from a curtain shop for the ends of blind cords.

Inside, each page is made separately, then attached back-to-back to its partner either by glueing or by sewing the two cloth-bound edges together all round. Textured paper was used for most of the pages; bought in assorted packs, it takes all kinds of paint, water-soluble coloured pencils, ink or crayon. It is especially useful for pen sketches, as the surface is more forgiving than smooth paper.

The front cover (top photograph) and reverse side (bottom photograph).

ST MARGARET (b. c. 1047), daughter of Edward the Exile and sister to the Aethling Edgar. She spent her first seven years in Hungary. In 1069, she married King Malcolm of Scotland. Her biographer, Turgot, writes of her, '... her chamber seemed to be a workshop of heavenly crafts. Always there were to be seen in it copes for the cantors, chasubles, stoles, altar cloths, as well as other priestly vestments and church ornaments. Some were in the course of preparation, others, already finished, were of admirable beauty. With these works she entrusted women of noble birth and approved conduct who were deemed worthy to be engaged in the Queen's service. No men were admitted among them, save such as she allowed to accompany her when she sometimes paid them a visit.'

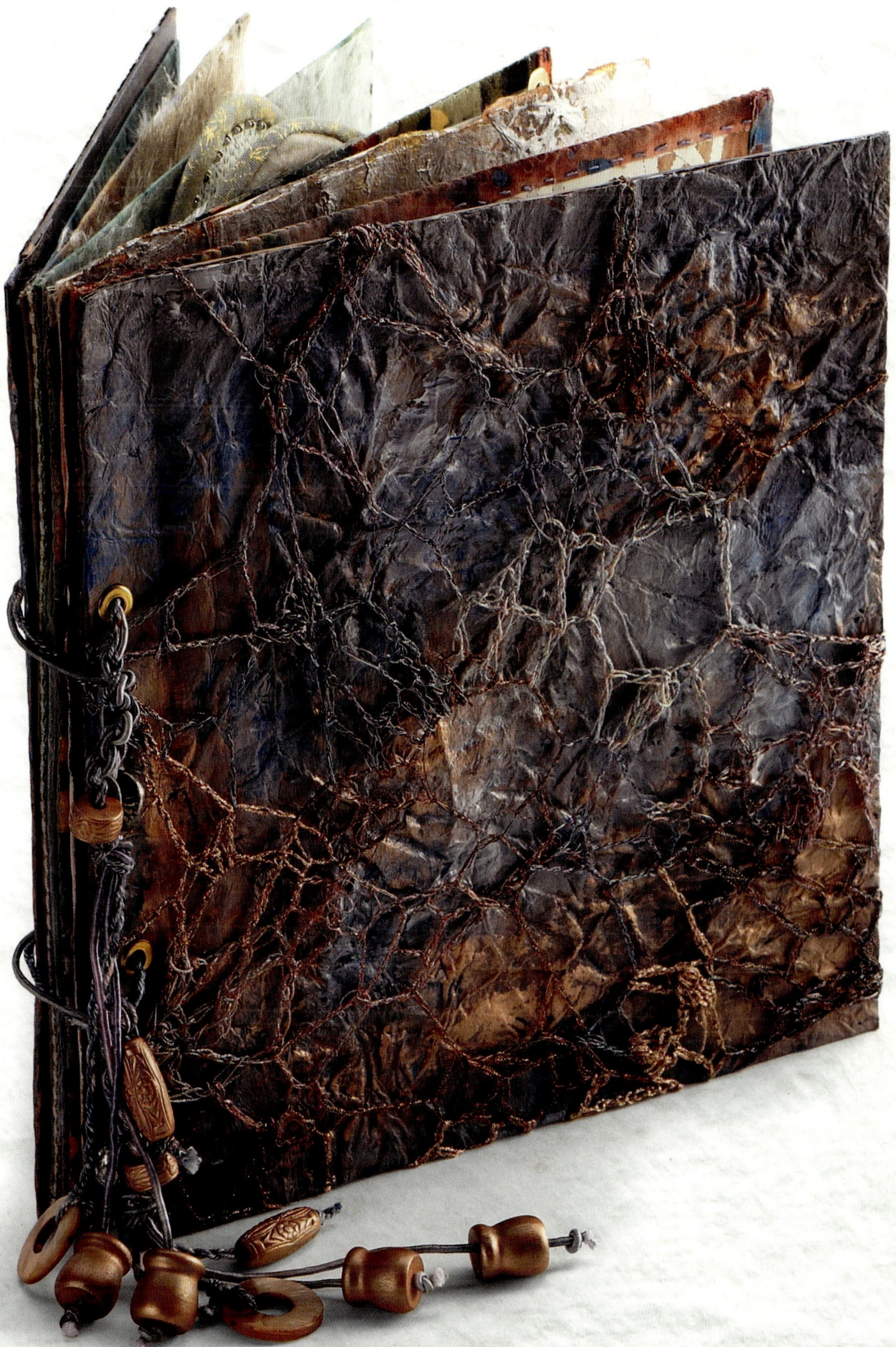
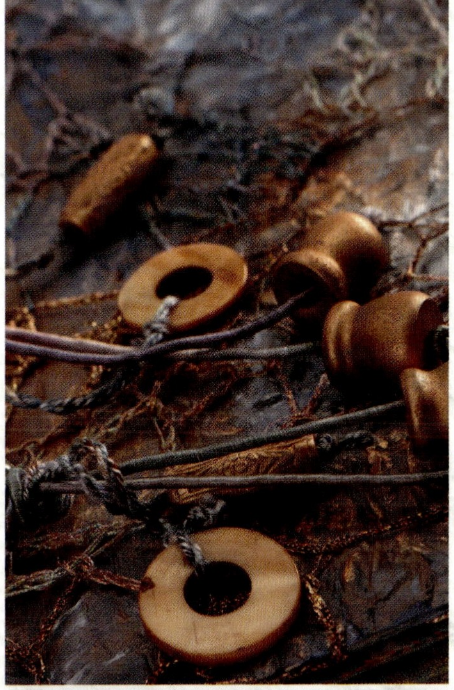
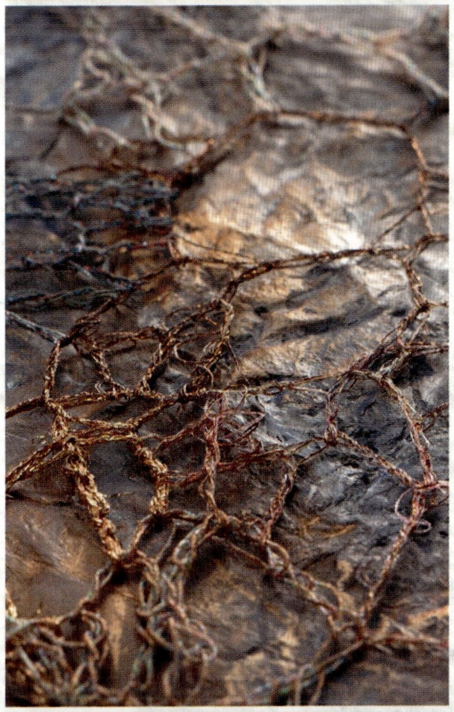
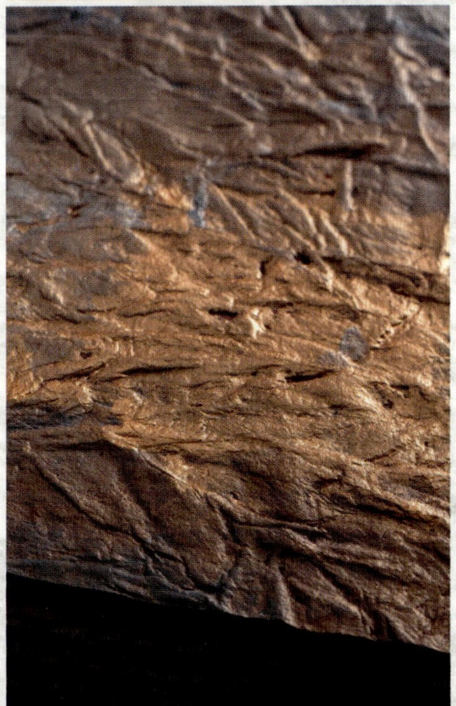

Inside front cover

Top left: a tiny backwards-facing dog engraved on a copper-alloy buckle plated with silver. Found in York. Like other examples on this page, backwards-facing animals are common to all three periods covered in this study, as they fit easily into a limited space.

Top centre: a letter 'd' from an early eleventh-century manuscript, probably painted at Winchcombe Abbey, Gloucestershire, and ornamented in the Norse Ringerike style.

Top right: a small eleventh-century tile originally from St Mary's Abbey (formerly the Nunnaminster) in Winchester. This shows a backwards-facing deer standing over a cross. This design was used for the embroidery seen at the beginning of The Bayeux Stitch Book (see page 54), and the original can be seen in the museum at Winchester.

Bottom left: animals facing each other in pairs with tongues meeting are often seen on Anglo-Saxon artefacts, like this example carved on a limestone cross-shaft at Codford-St-Peter in Wiltshire. They date from the late eighth century. Other similar tongue-touching animals can be seen on the border of the Bayeux Tapestry.

Bottom right: a limestone end-slab from an eleventh-century tomb found in St Paul's Churchyard, London, in 1852. Carved in the Norse Ringerike style, probably in England, it commemorates a follower of the Danish King Cnut with the Runic inscription, 'Ginna and Toki had this stone set up.' Popular at the time of Cnut, the Ringerike style is typified by animals from which tendrils emerge and scroll into a leafy ball. Although this stag appears to have claws, they are in fact exaggerated cloven hooves.

PAGE ONE

Top left: this bird appears on a tablet-woven braid of the eleventh century.

Top: the Uffington White Horse is carved into a steep chalk hillside, so large that one wonders how the poetic lines and perfect proportions could have been drawn by ancient Celts over two thousand years ago. An Iron-Age hill fort is situated on the hill-top above it. Formerly belonging to Berkshire, Uffington is now in Oxfordshire.

Centre left: a bird from the seventh-century Lindisfarne Gospels.

Centre right: entwined herons carved in the stone porch of the Anglo-Saxon church at Monkwearmouth (i.e. the monastery at the mouth of the River Wear) in Northumbria. What they mean or why they are there no one is sure.

Bottom: two necking swans appear on the borders of the Bayeux Tapestry embroidered in crewel wool on linen.

PAGE TWO
THE CALF OF MAN
CRUCIFIX

A part-reconstruction, which dates to the later eighth century, found on the Isle of Man and considered to be finer and more delicate than any other stone of the same period. Presumably, the missing figure on the right would have shown a soldier bearing a sponge on the end of a spear.

Page three
Celtic landscape

An evocation of moody metallic greys, moorland and heather-covered hills resounding to the grouse's warning calls, millstone-grit outcrops where boulders keep watch over bog and beck, ancient crosses and monastic cells where monks laboured over exquisite patterns of words: Northumbria.

Page four

From the Bayeux Tapestry, this tableau represents the funeral procession of King Eadward (the Confessor) on its way to Westminster Abbey in January 1066. The bier is covered by an embroidered pall spangled with rows of quatrefoils, and it is this design that inspired the small fragmentary embroidery seen on page 8.

QUEEN EMMA (d. 1052), second wife of King Cnut and mother of King Eadward the Confessor by her first husband King Aethelred, presented to Ely Cathedral 'a purple banner she had made, surrounded on every side by a border of gold embroidery, and adorned with magnificent embroidery of gold and precious gems … for her needlework seems to excel in work even her materials.'

LIBER ELIENSIS

EADWARDI : REGIS : AD : ECCLE

Page five

Casket shapes vary significantly, some meant to resemble buildings, all highly decorated and made of precious materials studded with gems, overlaid with gold.

Top left: an eighth-century reliquary from the region of Nijmegen in Belgium, in the shape of an altar shrine. It is small enough to have been hung round the neck of the owner, a Viking, perhaps as a container for relics. It is richly adorned with red amaldin and green glass set in gold.

Top right: the tenth-century Bamberg Casket. Made of gold, this casket has panels of walrus ivory intricately carved in the Mammen style. It is thought to have been the jewel box of Kunigunde, wife of the German Emperor Henry II.

Bottom left: the Rannveig Casket, a Scottish, Pictish or Irish reliquary of the eighth century. A Runic inscription on the base states that 'Rannveig owns this casket', showing that by the year 1000, the casket was in Norse hands when it may have been used as a jewel box.

Bottom right: the Cammin Casket is shaped like a house with gable ends, perhaps made as a reliquary in bronze-gilt with elk-antler panels decorated in Mammen-style carvings.

125

PAGE SIX
THE LEWIS CHESSMEN

The Isle of Lewis is an island in the Outer Hebrides where, in 1831 on the deserted Atlantic coastline, a hoard of carved walrus-ivory figures was discovered in a sandbank. Ninety-three pieces are known today, sixty-seven of which are chessmen. Most of these can now be seen in the British Museum. Measuring about 4in (10cm) high, the figures are thought to date somewhere beetween 1135 and 1170, judging by the mitres worn by the bishops. A little way outside our period, but almost certainly of Scandinavian origin. These two quilted panels show two sides of the same knight and are worked on calico with stab stitch and seeding.

126

PAGE SEVEN

127

Page eight

These distinctive matrons are derived from Viking amulets of silver-gilt and neilo measuring about 1½in (4cm) high. The lady on the left is from Uppland, Sweden, and dates from the sixth century, capturing perfectly the hauteur due to her seniority. Note her long hair tied in a knot, her large dish-brooch, and the trail of her gown.

The central figure is clearly old and wrinkled, dating from tenth-century Denmark and wearing a long, ornamented dress over a pleated chemise which she kicks into swirls as she walks. She holds her cloak with one hand, and wears her long hair knotted, like her companions.

The cup-bearing figure on the right is a Swedish Viking woman of the sixth century, probably representing a Valkyrie. Her dress is decorated with plaited and corded patterns, and she keeps her hair in a bun bound by a headband. Gold bracelets, earrings, neck-rings and a belt are her accessories.

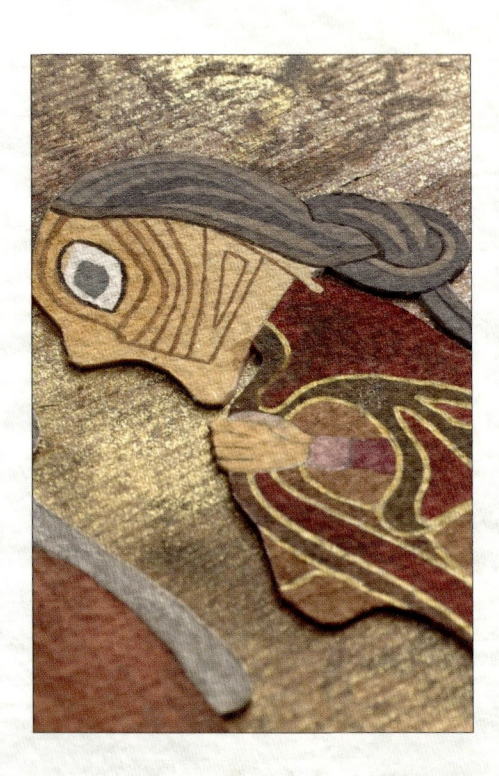

Page nine

Quilted samples of strapwork illustrate how random-dyed silk (at the top) and the reverse of a patterned cotton can add another dimension to a simple design. As with the chessmen design, random-dyed threads have been used for the seed-stitch backgrounds, though one is finer than the other.

129

Page ten

A sketch-page of motifs taken from coins, wrought ironwork, jewellery and book covers from the Celtic and Anglo-Saxon periods. Some of these are derived from complex designs which I have simplified, as the brooch in the bottom left-hand corner shows.

INSIDE BACK COVER

Boats and ships are a favourite Viking motif often found on coins and stone-carved monuments. These three are just some of those showing patterned sails, some striped, and rigging, although others have shields and figures, carved prows and weather vanes.

131

St Cuthbert project

My interest in the Great Northern Saints developed quite naturally from my love of early history and my northern roots. As I sifted through the abundance of material about the early Christian period, I had a feeling that the influence of these amazingly resilient people is as strong now as it was over one thousand years ago.

Cuthbert was born in 634 in the Scottish lowlands and became a monk at Melrose Abbey eighteen years later. He became guest-master at Ripon before being made Prior at Lindisfarne at the age of thirty. After ten years he became a hermit on the tiny, desolate island of Inner Farne but, after ten solitary years of devotion, he was persuaded to become Bishop of Lindisfarne, also known as Holy Island. His diocese encompassed the entire length of Hadrian's Wall, and his holiness and wisdom became legendary in his own lifetime. After two years as bishop, and much travelling, he gave up the bishopric in order to return to the Inner Farne, though not as a hermit. He died there on 20th March, 687, when his passing was signalled to the mainland by the waving of torches across the sea.

The seventh-century pectoral cross worn by St Cuthbert, made of gold with garnets and a central setting of garnet within a beaded collar surrounded by shells.

St Cuthbert of Lindisfarne

A small panel worked in appliqué and hand-stitchery, with the saint's pectoral cross at the right (seen opposite).
Private collection.

132

Though preferring to be buried on his island, he had agreed to be interred beside the high altar in the monastery at Lindisfarne, knowing that many would wish to visit his shrine. It was during these years that the Lindisfarne Gospels were written in his honour. But after continuous Viking raids that began in 796, it became clear that the monastery would not survive so, in 875, Cuthbert's shrine was taken off the island by all the inhabitants, during which the precious gospels were lost and found again.

The wanderers settled in Chester-le-Street where the relics remained until 995, and it was here where King Aethelstan made his donation of vestments as a mark of his friendship to the northerners. But Cuthbert's last resting-place was Durham, where a new church built on high ground on a loop in the river was safe from Viking raids. Later, his remains were interred behind the altar of the new cathedral built by the Normans in 1090, and now he rests not far from the Venerable Bede (673–735) who wrote Cuthbert's life using facts from those who knew him. His carved wooden coffin, his pectoral cross and gospel book can still be seen there, as can the magnificent embroideries.

These small figures of angels were taken from the saint's carved wooden coffin. This is now very broken up and difficult to decipher, but drawings have been made which show the four evangelists, the Virgin and Child, and several angels. The fabric used here is hand-dyed cotton.

The cover of St Cuthbert's own gospel book was made of red tooled leather with this design. The book is commonly known as the Stonyhurst Gospels since its acquisition by the Jesuit College at Stonyhurst in Lancashire, now on loan to Durham.

133

My project based on St Cuthbert, a long hanging and three matching cushions, was made by piecing together individually quilted sections that could be made on a small frame, taking up little space. The largest and first piece was the central figure: all others were added to this. This panel is made up of five pieces of fabric sewn together before quilting, and the transparency of the figure is achieved by painting parts of him with acrylic paint to lead colours from one area into the next. Coloured seeding of variegated threads washes over the background.

Ideas for the motifs came directly from a study of St Cuthbert's life as a hermit, from representations of him in manuscripts of the 1400s, and from the artefacts associated with him in Durham Cathedral. The relevance of the eider ducks at the top, for instance, is that they would lay their eggs in his footprints on the sand. The sea otters, shown in typical Celtic style, would wrap themselves around his feet to dry them after he had been standing in the sea to pray. The Viking ships allude to the brutal raids on Lindisfarne, and the symmetrical design between them is from the tooled leather cover of the saint's own gospel book which was found in his coffin. The lettering style is that used in the famous Lindisfarne Gospels, and the little figures on the cushions are taken from his coffin.

I used the reverse side of various printed cottons for my project, aiming for a sky-sea-sand colour-scheme with lots of plain calico to blend with the wall on which it hangs.

A medium-weight wadding (batting) was used between top and bottom layers of cotton. Stab stitch is used exclusively for the quilting, and although this sounds exceptionally monotonous, I found the rhythm of the stitching to be very therapeutic, requiring concentration whilst also allowing time for reflection. I attached the sections to each other by machine, working from the central panel outwards (see the diagram below), butting the wadding edge-to-edge, then overlapping the backing, stitching it in place by hand. Finally, all four edges were bound with long strips of fabric used on the panels, and the top edge was formed into loops to take the wooden hanging rod. I felt it was important to use a hanging device that reflected the era from which the design is taken. Stitched tassels and cords complete the hanging.

On the diagram below, the numbers show the order in which the pieces were assembled.

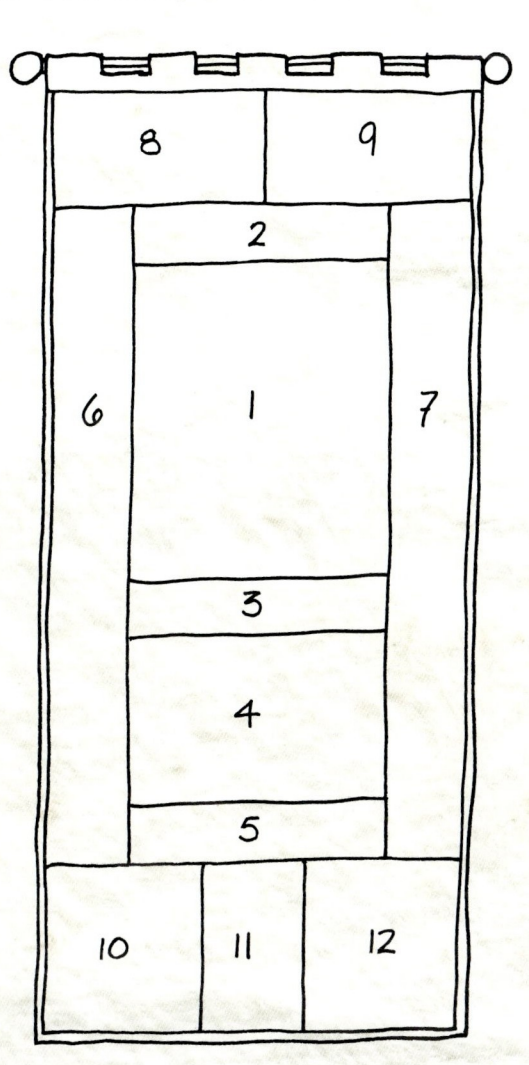

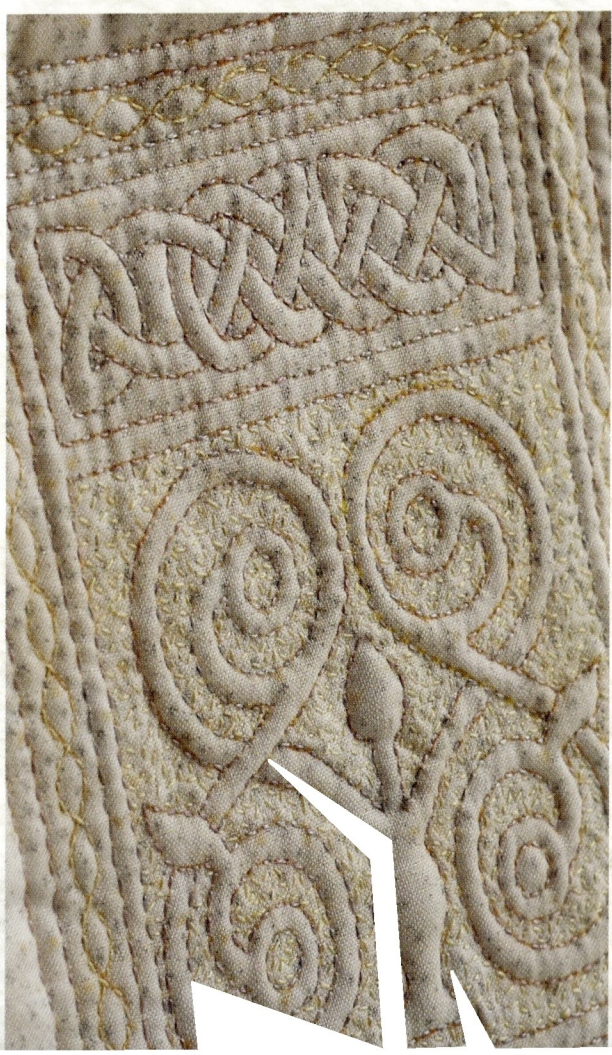

ST ALDHELM (d. 709/710), monk, scholar and first Bishop of Sherborne c. 675–709. Abbot of Malmesbury c. 674. Founded Wareham and Bradford-on-Avon. 'The shuttles, not filled with purple only but with various colours, are pushed here and there among the thick spreading threads, and then with the art of embroidery, they adorn all the woven-work with various groups of figures and images in different compartments.' To Abbess Hildalid of Barking in Essex, he wrote: '... satin underclothing ... scarlet tunics and hoods, sleeves with silk stripes, shoes edged with red fur, hair carefully arranged on forehead and temples with the curling iron, this is the modern habit. Dark veils yield to headdresses white and coloured, sewn with long ribbons and hanging to the ground; fingernails are sharpened, like talons of hawks or owls seeking their prey.'

E.S. DUCKETT, ANGLO-SAXON SAINTS AND SCHOLARS, LONDON, 1947

The figures of the Virgin and Child on this cushion (18 x 18in; 46 x 46cm) are taken from St Cuthbert's carved wood coffin. Worked in quilting and seeding on the reverse side of a colour-washed cotton surrounded by calico.

This is another saintly figure from St Cuthbert's coffin, first quilted on calico, then applied to a background of colour-washed cotton. This cushion measures 15 x 15in (38 x 38cm).

A viking-ship design from a coin of the period quilted on the reverse of a colour-washed cotton with an applied sail of striped cotton. The seeded background throws the boat into high relief. The wide calico border is made up of four separate pieces. This cushion measures 18 x 18in (46 x 46cm).

WILLIAM OF POITIERS, Norman chronicler of King William I: '… the splendour of the state robes, rich with embroidery of gold, wrought by English hands, taken back by Chief William and his nobles, made all that France and Normandy has beheld of the same seem mean by comparison.'

William of Poitiers describes how 'King Harold went into battle carrying a banner embroidered with a fighting man worked in gold and enriched with precious stones.' Also, 'The women of England are very skilful in needlework and the working of gold lace, and the men are distinguished in all the arts.'

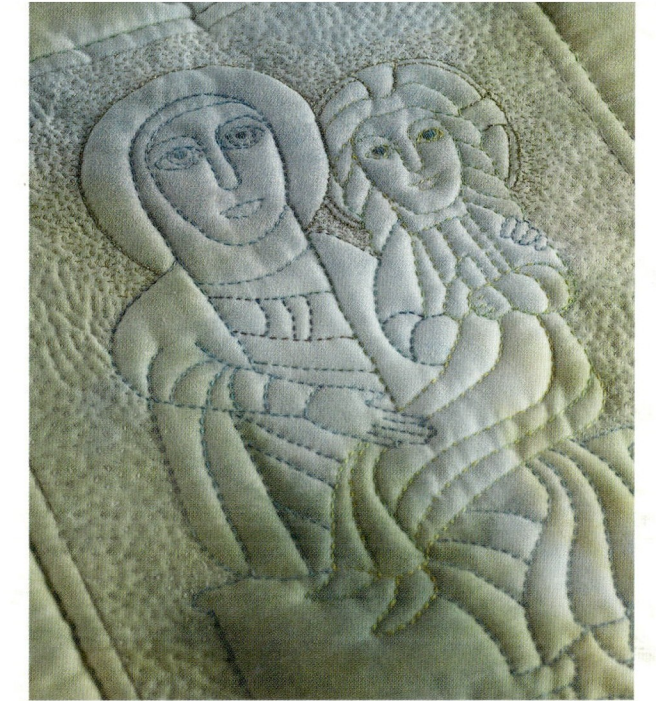

Domesday Book

Introduction

Soon after William of Normandy became King of England in 1066, he ordered a survey of all towns and villages to find out what land he owned, what people and property, and what taxes would be due to him. He sent officials into every part of his kingdom and, in two years, scribes had made an inventory which came to be called Domesday Book and which still exists in its original form. Most of the places in Domesday can still be found today, like the tiny village of Oakley in Buckinghamshire, which had been given to one of William's followers, Robert de Tosny, who leased it to Robert Fitzwalter.

To embroiderers, the interest lies particularly in an Anglo-Saxon lady named Aelfgyth who was an expert in gold embroidery and who was given land by the county sheriff on condition that she taught his daughter how to do it. Perhaps she had several pupils. My text on these four embroidered 'pages' has been abridged to make it fit.

The four-page Book measures 7½ x 7in (19 x 18cm) when closed, and is made up of eight panels mounted over medium-weight Vilene, then stitched back-to-back. I used commercial cotton fabrics for these and, to create an uneven edge, I back-stitched a wobbly line round each panel before painting the outer edge with a colour that matched the tabs. Thick watercolour works well for this, using a fine brush or, alternatively, acrylic paint. The paint must not be too wet, or it will leach into the adjoining areas.

Trapped between the panels are short tubes of folded fabric spaced to fit with its neighbour, one between the other. These tubes were glued lightly in place before the panels were sewn together. The two ends have continuous tubes.

The panels are held together by a hinge system where a smooth stick of bamboo (cheap chopsticks are ideal for this) slides down through the tubes. The base of the stick is stuck into a large-eyed flat bead (for the feet) and the top finished off with a matching bead. Gold cord was stitched all round the front and back covers and the two ends hung with cords and reels of gold threads meant to represent Aelfgyth's profession. These reels were made from gold-painted card tubes.

The two houses on the covers are adapted from those seen on the Bayeux Tapestry. One of them is embroidered in gold threads, felt and beads, the other in coloured silks using stem, satin, Bayeux stitch and French knots.

The original text is in a mixture of Latin and Old English, and my lettering style is based on that of the Bayeux Tapestry, worked entirely in back-stitch.

The front of the Book (top photograph) is mostly appliqué, and the reverse side (bottom photograph) is worked entirely in stitchery.

NE · ARE ·
ORDARS
SLAVES
OR · 200
E · NOT
PARK · IN ·
C · THE ·
TED · HER
E · WAS
ONDITION
ING · HIS
GOLD ·
· WORK

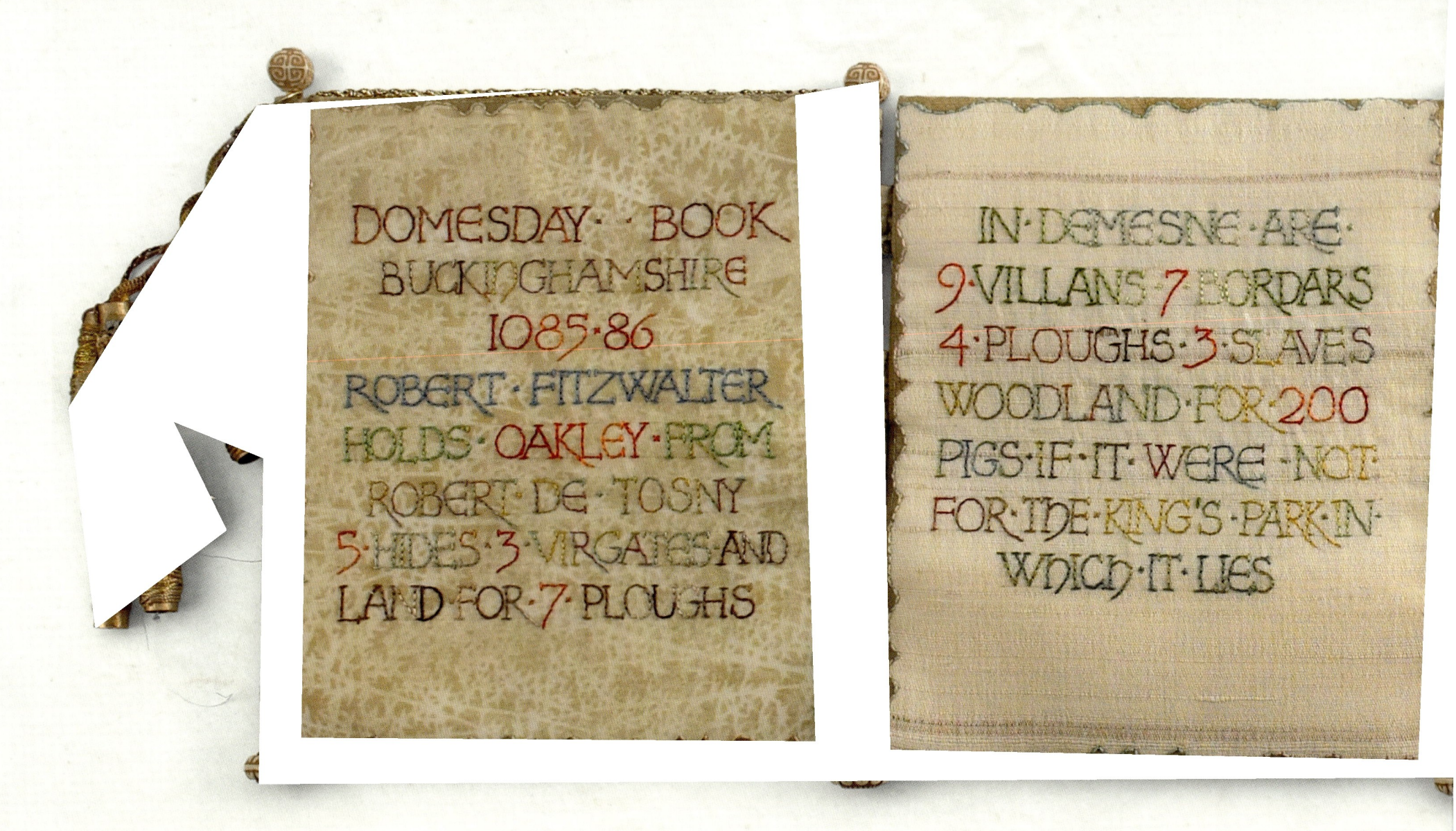

DOMESDAY BOOK
BUCKINGHAMSHIRE
1085–86
ROBERT FITZWALTER
HOLDS OAKLEY FROM
ROBERT DE TOSNY
5 HIDES 3 VIRGATES AND
LAND FOR 7 PLOUGHS

IN DEMESNE (i.e. the lord's private land) ARE
9 VILLANS 7 BORDARS (smallholders)
4 PLOUGHS 3 SLAVES
WOODLAND FOR 200
PIGS IF IT WERE NOT
FOR THE KING'S PARK IN
WHICH IT LIES

QUEEN EDGYTH (d. 1075), wife of Eadward the Confessor, sister to King Harold of England who was killed in 1066. According to the chronicler William of Malmesbury, Queen Edith embroidered with her own hands the robes worn by her husband at festivals. She was a skilled embroiderer.

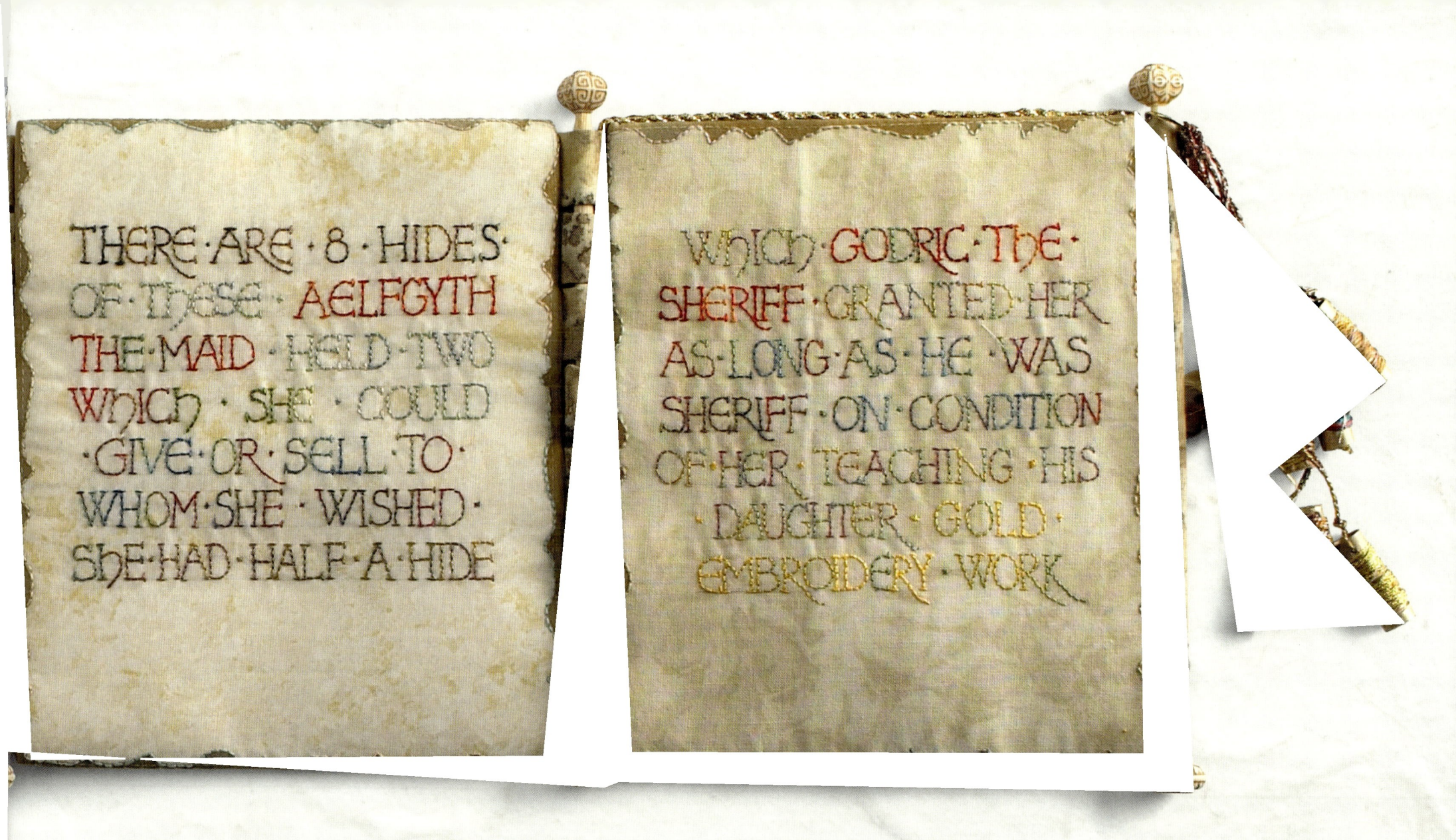

THERE ARE 8 HIDES (a unit of land sufficient to
maintain a family)
OF THESE AELFGYTH
THE MAID HELD TWO
WHICH SHE COULD
GIVE OR SELL TO
WHOM SHE WISHED
SHE HAD HALF A HIDE

WHICH GODRIC THE
SHERIFF GRANTED HER
AS LONG AS HE WAS
SHERIFF ON CONDITION
OF HER TEACHING HIS
DAUGHTER GOLD
EMBROIDERY WORK

According to Domesday Book, three great royal manors in Bedfordshire owed annual dues to Queen Edith of gold and ad opus reginae (for the queen's work). Leighton owed two ounces and so did Houghton. Luton owed four ounces. Wool for embroidery threads may have come from Edith's own flock of sheep on lands in Cirencester, Gloucestershire, which was later acquired by Queen Mathilde.

Index

A

Anglo-Saxon 9, 10, 12, 14, 16, 22, 25, 30, 33, 36, 37, 43, 50, 52, 54, 56, 59, 62, 69, 72, 82, 86, 90, 100, 104, 105, 106, 116, 117, 121, 130
animals
  birds 121
  cattle 62
  Celtic 71, 120, 121
  deer 54, 120
  eider duck 134, 135
  horse (Lewis Chessmen) 127
  Iron-age horse 121
  jet animals 100
  Ringerike deer 120
  sea otter 134, 135

B

Baltic Sea 101
Battle of Hastings 15, 117
Bayeux Tapestry 8, 15, 33, 36, 42, 46, 47, 52, 54, 55, 70–73, 78, 116, 120, 121, 124, 138–141
Bayeux Tapestry Finale 82, 83
Beads and findings 4, 5, 10, 11, 16, 17, 21, 28, 29, 34–37, 44, 45, 52, 53, 66, 67, 74–83, 87, 90, 91, 96–98, 100–103, 106, 111, 118, 119, 138–141
Bedfordshire 141
Belgium 14, 15, 125
Beowulf 4, 15
Black Sea 101
Boats and ships 84, 85, 131, 137
Book-making 9, 10, 16, 37, 44, 45, 52, 74, 97, 110, 111, 118, 138
Bosham 42
Braids and cords 5, 20, 28, 29, 34, 74, 79, 80, 87, 97–99, 105, 111, 138, 139
Byrhtnoth/Battle of Maldon 15, 71
Britain 12, 36, 100, 101, 105
British Museum 64, 126, 127
Bronze Age 13, 20, 34, 98
Buckinghamshire 37, 92, 138, 140
Byzantium 36, 74

C

caskets 125
Canterbury 32, 33
Celtic/Celts 10, 12–14, 16, 20, 22, 23, 25, 28, 29, 52, 59, 64, 84, 106, 112, 121, 123, 129, 130, 135
churches
  Holy Trinity, Caen 88
  St Lawrence, Bradford-on-Avon 56
  St Paul's, Jarrow 52, 69
  St Peter's, Monkwearmouth 121
collage 63, 65, 67, 78–83, 90, 91
Cornwall 12, 13
costumes/garments 13, 14, 32, 34, 36, 37, 46, 47, 74, 76–83, 87, 90, 91–96, 104, 106, 107, 116, 117, 128, 135

D

Denmark 13, 15, 20, 34, 36, 100, 101, 120, 125, 128
Domesday Book 15, 33, 90, 91, 92, 138–141
Durham 14, 15, 95, 116, 133, 135
dyeing 26, 27, 55, 96

E

Ely (Cambs.) 71, 89, 94, 112
embroiderers 12, 13, 15, 95, 98
  Aelfflaed 71
  Aelfgifu of Northampton 32
  Aelfgyth 92, 138–141
  Aelthelswith (Lady) 112
  Eanswitha 15
  Leofgyth of Knook 33
  Mahalt 104
  St Etheldreda 94
  St Margaret 118
  Wulfwynn (Abbess) 33
Egypt 22, 100

F

fabrics
  canvas 36, 68, 95, 111, 117
  cotton 22, 42, 126, 127, 129, 133–141
  felt 16, 74, 75, 82, 91, 110–115, 117
  fur 23
  hessian (burlap) 16, 36
  lace 23, 76, 98
  leather 23, 104, 116
  linen 28, 29, 36, 43, 50, 51, 54, 62, 77, 86
  muslin 23, 117
  silk 12, 23, 31, 34, 36, 50, 76, 92–97, 106, 107, 112–115, 117, 129
  Vilene 11, 37, 73, 97, 112–115
  wool 23, 84
Far East 101
France 14, 46, 88, 95

G

gemstones 100, 101
Germany 13, 125
Gloucestershire 120, 141
Gospel books 32, 110
  Durrow 84
  Kells 84
  Initial letter 120
  Lindisfarne 121, 133
  Stonyhurst 133

H

Hadrian's Wall 84, 132
Hampshire 33, 36
Hems and seams 34, 36, 49, 50, 51
Hungary 24, 118

I

Iceland 18
Ireland 12, 15, 64, 84, 98, 100, 125
Iron Age 12, 13, 121
Isle of Lewis Chessmen 11, 126, 127
Isle of Man 101, 122
Isle of Wight 37
Italy 100

142

J

jewellery 20, 30, 44, 45, 47, 130

K

Kent 37
Kings
  Athelred 15
  Aethelstan 32, 95, 133
  Cnut 15, 112, 120
  Eadward the Confessor 4, 8, 9, 33, 92, 124, 141
  Edward the Exile 118
  Harold 116, 117, 141
  Malcolm of Scotland 118
  Oswald of Northumbria 74
  Wiglaf 57
  William 33, 82, 95, 117, 138
Knook (Wilts.) 33

L

Language
  Latin 13, 140
  Old English 13, 15, 116, 140
Lincolnshire 100
London 120

M

Malmesbury 95, 141
Modelling clay 72, 73, 83, 101–103

N

Near East 36
Normans/Normandy 12, 14, 15, 18, 33, 36, 52, 73, 82, 95, 96, 133, 138
North Africa 36
Norway 13, 15, 22, 36, 64, 120, 125

O

Opus Anglicanum 15
Oseberg 15, 22, 36, 64

P

paint, use of 16, 18, 19, 20, 26–29, 31, 34, 37, 44, 45, 52, 53, 63, 65, 71, 80, 81, 97, 110, 118, 119, 135, 138

Q

Queens
  Edgyth (Edith) 15, 33, 36, 92, 141
  Emma 89, 112
  Kunigunde (Germany) 125
  Margaret (Scotland) 118
  Mathilde 33, 141

R

Ripon (Yorks.) 47, 132
Rome/Romans 12, 13, 36, 100
Romsey (Hants.) 33
Runes 18, 19, 120, 125

S

Saints
  Aldhelm 135
  Cuthbert 14, 15, 37, 94, 95, 132–137
  Dunstan 12, 32
  Harlindis and Relindis 15
  Matthew 135
Scandinavia 13, 15, 50, 87
Scotland 12, 15, 125, 132
Spain 36
stitches
  back 138–141
  Bayeux 8, 9, 11, 34, 52–71, 106, 107, 120, 138
  buttonhole 34, 35, 43, 49, 55–57, 87
  Ceylon 48, 49
  chain 34, 43, 49, 107, 116
  feather 34, 35, 49, 76, 77
  French knots 16, 138
  herringbone 34, 35, 49, 50, 66, 77, 81, 106
  long and short 11, 60
  running/whipped running 8, 16, 21, 34–37, 43, 44, 48, 49, 55, 88, 89
  satin 8, 9, 36, 70, 81, 97, 138
  seeding 126, 127, 129, 134–137
  split 34, 43, 49, 50
  stem/outline 8, 34, 36, 37, 43, 44, 58, 60, 106, 116, 138
Suffolk 37
Sutton Hoo 64
Sweden 13, 15, 34, 101, 128
Switzerland 12

T

tassels/fringes 5, 13, 20, 21, 28, 29, 36, 44, 45, 96–98, 106, 107, 111, 113, 134

techniques
- appliqué 8, 11, 20, 34, 36, 42, 70, 72, 74, 93–95, 107, 116, 132, 138
- canvaswork 68, 95, 111
- couching/laidwork 11, 34, 37, 44, 49, 52, 66, 67, 93, 106, 116
- darning 36, 37, 45, 117
- goldwork 11, 15, 34, 36, 37, 73, 86, 112–115
- knitting/crochet 117–119
- knotting/netting 15, 34, 116
- nalebinding 34, 48
- needlelace 34, 48, 49
- needleweaving 22, 23, 111, 117
- patchwork 70, 71
- quilting 34, 35, 46, 47, 93, 94, 110, 126, 127, 129, 133–137
- tablet weaving 30, 31, 36, 37, 84, 87–89, 121
- weaving/spinning 24, 25, 36

textiles 13–16, 34, 36, 48, 73, 76–78, 92–95, 102, 103

tools 16, 25, 30, 31, 104, 112

threads 98, 99
- cotton 11, 54, 58, 59, 61, 70, 86, 95, 106, 107, 126, 127, 138–141
- gold 11, 14, 30, 34, 37, 70, 86, 89, 93, 95–97, 106, 112–115, 138, 139
- linen 11, 26, 30, 87–89
- silk 12, 66, 87, 89
- string 23, 67, 105
- wool 23, 26, 30, 36, 54, 68, 87–89, 111, 117
- yarns 66, 67, 117

V

Venerable Bede 69, 133
Vikings 10, 12, 14, 15, 18, 34, 36, 37, 48, 50, 86, 87, 96, 100, 101, 104, 105, 116, 128, 131, 133, 135, 137

W

Wales 12, 36
Wiltshire 33, 120
Winchester 15, 33, 54, 88, 95, 116, 120
Whitby jet 101

Y

York 15, 30, 34, 74, 100, 116